Best Wishes

Dan Phelan

Success,
Happiness,
Independence

SUCCESS
HAPPINESS,
INDEPENDENCE

Own Your Own Business

Donald J. Phelan

Glenbridge Publishing Ltd.

Library of Congress Catalog Card Number: LC 94-79175

International Standard Book Number: 0-944435-31-9

Printed in the U. S. A.

CONTENTS

Introduction

Congratulations. You have just turned the first page in what may be a very exciting and rewarding chapter in your life. Dynamic people are those who realize life has much to offer and know good things happen to those who are willing to go after their dreams. Because there are so many choices, we often get confused and frustrated in not knowing what we really want, what's available, or how to pursue our goals.

This book will give you insight into how successful business owners have dealt with the same anxieties you may now be experiencing, and moved on to be successful in the world of business. But you might find yourself thinking, "If it's that easy, why isn't everybody doing it?" My answer is, I really don't know. Owning your own business offers the best opportunity for wealth, independence, and security of any other choice you could make. Fear of the unknown or failure is certainly a factor that keeps many from taking the plunge. But in interviewing over thirty successful business owners who were willing to share their experiences and offer advice, I concluded that succeeding in business just isn't that difficult if you are willing to learn from the success of others!

Much has been written about the small business community and the struggle to succeed. Some of the information is presented by bankers, accountants, professors, attorneys, and professional writers, many of whom I classify as "spectators." You can often recognize their work by the snappy titles they use, such as: "12 Steps to Success," or "10 Things to Watch For," or "7 Questions to Ask."

But what about the players? What do the people who have realized their cherished dream have to say? The material for this book was developed after talking with successful business owners and observing their styles and techniques. These were not the industrial giants, but the small business owners who started with little more than a dream and a strong desire to succeed. Not surprisingly, they all agree on some fundamental concepts, none of which are terribly complicated, nor will you find them in any textbook.

Many of the names of the owners have been changed to protect their privacy, but without their candor and willingness to share, this book would not have been possible.

From my own personal experience, I'm convinced of two things: owning your own successful business just isn't that difficult, and it offers the best chance for attaining personal satisfaction.

1

Are You Ready For a Change?

Going into business for yourself, particularly the first time, is fraught with conflicting feelings of excitement, enthusiasm, anxiety, and nervousness. You would be the exception if you weren't experiencing various levels and combinations of these emotions.

The decision to go into your own business might be one of the most monumental events in your life. I would offer you this bit of advice as you wrestle with this decision—learn what you can from other business owners who have already been down the road and are willing to share their insights. You will discover two things: many of their business tips are not generally found in textbooks, and they are more willing to talk and share than you would have imagined.

Knowing just where to start, whom to talk with, and what questions to ask can be awkward. Observing this

3

"getting started" process for a number of years, I have concluded there are some preliminary considerations that neophyte entrepreneurs normally confront before going into their own business, namely:

1. What are the risks in making a career change?

2. What skills are necessary for succeeding in business?

3. What can I expect?

Change can be stressful, particularly if the change is imposed upon you by someone else. Conversely, when you are the one initiating the change, it can result in a positive challenge and a significant sense of relief. Let's start right now with the premise that you are going to seize control and make the difficult decisions that will produce a meaningful change in your life.

During the years I worked in corporate America, one thing that distressed me the most was listening to people grumble about their jobs, the boss, and the "idiots" they had to work with. When you would ask them why they didn't quit and do something else, the answer always was the same: "I would like to but I can't." Then came the litany of excuses: "We just bought a new house." "The kids are in college." "I can't afford to give up the benefits." "I've been here too long." "I can't make this kind of money." Over the years I've watched these same people slowly die inside by becoming bitter, angry, and frustrated. So, the price we pay for not making changes can often be devastating. Failure to deal with frustrating issues, in any part of our life, can result in a cancerous affliction. The disgruntled employee can become the tense parent or the insecure spouse.

It is satisfying to hear about the employees of United Airlines who have taken over the ownership of the company. That re-enforces the notion that people want an active role in the decisions that affect their work, and they do have a genuine need for exercising some control over their future. On a smaller scale, it is quite common for an individual employee to take over the ownership of his or her employer's business and then generally do well at making the business even more successful. Owning your own business is one of the few remaining ways we have of using our individualism to produce both a livelihood and personal satisfaction. In few other endeavors is there as much potential for financial success and a sense of purpose than that of owning your own business.

The American dream need not be just a dream. Thousands of others, just like yourself, have moved from dream to reality by simply making the decision to take control of their lives. As a starting point in your search for independence and success, spend some time considering these questions:

1. Where am I now?

2. Where would I like to be?

3. How can I get there?

4. Why do I want to go?

Let's examine the first question—Where am I now? You may not spend much time thinking about this. But you are a unique and special person. There isn't another living person who has had the same life experiences as you. These experiences have helped shape your current values and beliefs. So what's the big deal, you ask? Well, what have *you* done lately to tap this special resource.

Your unique characteristics, if focused properly and leveraged to your advantage, could easily result in significant personal satisfaction and monetary gain. Or they could be used by someone else. It seems to me the choice is simple—would you like to begin working for your benefit instead of someone else's?

As the world's economic structures change, we hear more discussion about the absence of job satisfaction, adequate compensation, security, and a whole basketful of other things that we didn't worry too much about a few years ago. Job security is no longer something we can take for granted as an earned benefit that is given in exchange for years of loyal employment. In these times of corporate restructuring, downsizing, and increasing global competition, there is much cause for concern.

We have seen thousands of people lose their jobs in the past several years, with the likelihood of more to come. And many of the more "fortunate" ones who are still employed now face a new challenge. Job descriptions are being changed to help facilitate this restructuring, which often translates into retraining and additional responsibilities of the remaining workers. Many claim this is necessary for the nation to maintain a productive work force. While that may be so, the changes may not be good if you are being pushed in a direction you don't want to go. Taking stock of where you are should be pretty straightforward. But the more relevant question that needs to be answered is: have *you* actively charted the course that brought you to this point, or have other forces been more responsible? Who is looking out for your best interests? If you can answer that, then you can answer, "Where am I now?"

Now let's look at "where you would like to be." Most of us want the same things in life: security, independence, respect, a sense of contribution, and a chance at the good life. Unless you've inherited wealth, the good life must be earned by working.

The question of "where you would like to be" is always more difficult to answer. People in search of "something better" will spend more time on this single issue than anything else. The problem is not knowing all of the alternatives and what qualifications are needed. There are a couple of different ways to approach this question. The first is to list those things you don't like, such as the weather, heavy work, city life, boring work, dealing with people, being supervised, etc. This method helps us identify those things you don't like and provides motivation for a change. But, unfortunately, it falls short of helping us select what we really want. In the following chapters we will spend more time finding a solution to this perplexing question by examining some of the alternatives and asking business people to share their views with us.

For now, just reflect on your current position and ask yourself these questions: Will you find yourself in the future with a career that provides job satisfaction, growth potential, and adequate financial compensation? Or will you simply be competing with thousands of other workers for whatever positions are available? Will you be able to apply your uniqueness and allow your work to become an extension of yourself? Or will you just become a small player for someone else in a large impersonal game and just be "putting in your time"?

Thinking of the future usually means dreaming to most of us. But planning and making dreams come true is what distinguishes the successful business owner from the idle daydreamer. Setting a reasonable goal is extremely important. If your goal is to be "exceedingly rich" in five years with little or no effort, your best chance might be to go out and win the lottery. But many people, including yourself, can set reasonable goals and attain them with nothing more than focus, effort, and determination.

I counseled a young couple who had spent several years working in the motel business, he as a handyman and she as a clerk and maid. They felt that their experiences, personalities, and willingness to work hard qualified them as excellent motel owners (the vision). I was in total agreement and couldn't help but be impressed by their drive and enthusiasm. The owner of the motel where they both worked had mentioned in passing that she would like to sell her motel sometime soon. That was all they needed to hear. They were certainly in the right spot at the right time. Together, they had frequently discussed the improvements they would make, if only they owned the motel. The restaurant, which was a part of the motel, was being leased to someone else for the ridiculously low amount of $200 per month. The couple would take over the restaurant and turn it into a real profit center. There also were two units that had been converted into a storage room for broken-down furniture. This would make an excellent area for a conference room that could be offered to the local business clubs, or perhaps even an area for Sunday brunches or catered banquets.

The potential seemed unlimited. They had saved about $15,000 to invest in a business. The owner wanted $330,000 for the motel and wasn't interested in doing any owner financing. So the couple headed to a local bank where the outcome was quite predictable. The bank was willing to loan 70 percent of the asking price, about $230,000, and wanted the couple to come up with $100,000.

For hours we discussed some of the financial alternatives in the hope that they could find a way, not only to buy the motel, but also to fund the improvements they felt so strongly about. We calculated an offering price that we thought represented a fair market value and developed a strategy for convincing the owner that it would be in her best interest to get involved in the long-term financing.

The next few days were quite distressing for the young couple as neither the owner nor the bank showed any signs of compromising. The story does have a happy ending, however. Persistence and a real commitment to their long-term goal kept the couple on track for something they could afford. They finally located a four-plex that was in need of tender loving care, and it was in their price range. That was more than three years ago. Today, their equity in that unit is about $35,000, and as you might have guessed, they are still looking for their own motel and won't rest until they find it.

In the case of this couple, owning a motel is a dream. Buying the four-plex was simply a step toward fulfilling that dream. Dreams always seem to be a part of our lives. But the difference between the casual daydream and the attainable vision is your commitment to take action. So now you need to ask the question, "How can I get there?" Taking the first step is always the most difficult. Begin by putting some dimensions on your vision. For example, is this something I would be capable of doing, and is my timing right? How much money will be required, and what precautions should I take to protect my investment? What is the growth potential for both the business and myself?

Your initial dream might be very specific and detailed, or it may be a little vague and difficult to explain. In either case, it will be important to develop short-range and inter-mediate goals. Start now by keeping a written record of your goals and plans, and refer to them often. Don't hesi-tate to make updates and modifications as you acquire more information. The more specific the goals, the more compre-hensive the action plan will be—and the more likely your chance of success.

Try testing the water. Talk with others, particularly those who may be directly affected by your actions and whose support you will certainly need. Seek the opinion of others and weigh the consequences of making a change versus doing nothing. Make sure that you always consider any glaring obstacles to achieving your dream. For example, the expense of a son or daughter's college education is something to factor into the earnings projection when weighing investment opportunities. Undoubtedly, you have heard of the failure rates of small businesses, and those statistics can be quite frightening, and should be. But let me assure you, if you permit your intuition (uniqueness) to set the direction, and let your good sense handle the planning, you will increase your probability of success immensely. In other words, let your heart handle the vision, and your mind handle the plans.

Recently, a businessman was telling me about an opportunity he had to purchase a popular nightclub at a very attractive price. He said there were three reasons for deciding against it—he was not a night person, he hated loud music, and he didn't feel comfortable around younger people. This would be a case where the heart rejected the idea and spared the mind the task of developing a plan.

After your vision has survived the test of scrutiny, then it's time to start taking action. Begin by formulating some short-term, positive steps. Form the habit of writing things down. When you define a particular action item—include the date when you expect it to be completed, who is responsible for taking the action, and how will success be measured. This written record will provide a data base that you will find invaluable as time goes on. For example, an action item list might look something like this:

Action Item	Date	Who	Success
1. Talk with banker regarding need for a business plan	7-25	Don	Guidelines and suggested format
2. Call zoning department	7-28	Sue	Can we open a bakery at this location?

It is at this point in the process where many would-be business owners begin to falter and have second thoughts about going into business. After all, this is beginning to sound like work. Keeping records and writing things down may not be your comfort zone, and it certainly isn't what you thought running a business would be like. Those who have succeeded before you have consistently demonstrated the ability to move from a vision to a reality by formulating specific plans and developing a course of action. While there are a few gifted people who trust everything to memory and write little or nothing down on paper, the majority of successful business owners have developed the habit of keeping a written record, not only for planning and historical purposes, but to assist them in explaining their position to bankers, attorneys, or their employees. Documenting your activities can be done informally using a pocket calendar or as detailed as you feel necessary. But it is time well spent. If you are feeling reluctant and less enthusiastic with the prospect of owning your own business, then now is the time to re-examine your motivation for making a change. The skills to succeed in business can be quite different from those needed to work for someone else. Shifting from "worker only" to "manager-worker" is a transition that many do not make easily, and can lead to failure in business.

Before you set goals for yourself and establish a plan of action, ask yourself, "why do I want to change?" Going into business is not for everyone, and there certainly is no shame in recognizing that this may not be "your cup of tea." Owning your own business takes dedication, perseverance, patience, and long hours of work. Are you going after something you want, or are you running away from what you don't want? Perhaps you are doing a little of both. Too often when we feel trapped, we simply shrug our shoulders and resign ourselves to the status quo—even if that is a life of mediocrity. Removing yourself from that quagmire may be the first step toward freedom and prosperity. Remember that dynamic people take charge; they go after what they want and are willing to pay the price. Don't give in to the temptation of resignation or that feeling of helplessness. When you become a business owner, you will find there are many new hurdles for you to overcome. To succeed, you must be willing to accept the challenge of change, or learn to be content with your present state.

There are no right or wrong reasons for changing a career path, but if you don't understand the purpose of the change, you certainly will have a hard time recognizing success. Making a change or doing something different can certainly be uncomfortable and requires a great deal of staying power. You will find it is worth the effort only if the results are meaningful. In other words, if you meet or exceed your goals, then it's a successful venture. You don't want to go into your own business with anything less than total commitment to your goals and plans and with confidence in your ability to see it through.

Each of us measures satisfaction differently, but for the most part it is based on expectations and goals. If your goal were to make a lot of money, and that didn't happen, then you would probably say that going into business wasn't worth it, even though you may have had other positive experiences. It would have been a real treat to have been able to sit down and talk business with Sam Walton, the founder of Wal-Mart. He had said that he had no idea that he would end up making the money that he did. He measured his success by offering a family-oriented business that specialized in friendly service at competitive prices. I suspect that creating great wealth was not a major consideration when he first started.

There is nothing wrong with going into business for the purpose of making money. If you look at the ten wealthiest people in the world, or even the fifty wealthiest, you won't find any of them working for someone else. However, I would be surprised to hear many of them say that making a great fortune was their primary motivation for going into business, at least initially. Of course, if you select the shipbuilding or publication business, you will probably be in a better position to make a fortune than if you start with a hobby shop. Although Debbi Fields did pretty well with her cookies. The founder and owner of Mrs. Fields Cookies stated recently on PBS television that she started her multimillion dollar business in the kitchen of her home. She began with two underlying beliefs: She could make cookies that were good to eat, and going into business was something she knew she had to try. Bankers wouldn't give her the time of day, but they would eat the cookies she offered. She was a very determined person and decided that "no" was not an acceptable answer. Her persistence paid off when a banker granted a small loan to get her started. Today her main advice to entrepreneurs is, "don't ever give up."

The goal most often mentioned by successful business owners is the desire to gain independence. People who have strong value systems tend to resist compromise and find that their real comfort zone is when they make decisions and influence outcomes. Entrepreneurs usually rank this sense of independence and uniqueness above all other reasons for going into business. Your reasons for going into your own business are very personal and need not be defended—just understood.

Now that we have reflected on the four questions relating to change, it would be beneficial if we could identify any specific skill or characteristic that successful business owners had when they first started. And since our future could be reflected in their past—they could share some of the problems that we may encounter along the way. What might we expect that we are now unaware of?

When you meet business owners and they describe the operation of their businesses or give you a tour, you're usually a little bit in awe and very impressed. You may think to yourself that you could never master the things they have. But if you spend time with them and get them to talk about the days when they were getting started, you will find something much different. When they took their personal inventory, did they have all the skills they now possess? Were they smarter than the average bear? One owner told me he didn't think the real smart people ever went into business for themselves—just the brave and restless!

I have discovered that, in most cases, people who go into business for themselves do so with few of the polished skills displayed by successful owners. But most come in due time. You will discover that many of the so-called lofty concepts, such as market penetration and just-in-time inventory, are all touted with much fanfare. But on close examination, they just intuitively make good sense and really aren't that complicated. The successful business owner has learned to use good sense in mastering business concepts and tools.

Many years ago I came to know a remarkable couple who founded and managed a successful printing company in Denver, Colorado. In talking with them, I can recall asking how two people could develop such a successful business in less than twenty years. They paused, looking somewhat confused, and said, "you just work hard and live within your means." I must say I was expecting much more, a unique marketing strategy, an inventory control process, a dynamic cash management program, or something even more definitive.

Much later I realized that they were a couple who shared the same dream, worked extremely well together, and had the ability of focusing on doing the little things well. They knew how to work hard, but more importantly, they knew how to work on the right things at the right time. For example, when sales were soft, they would apply all of their efforts to first understanding the problem and then to finding a solution. They were very methodical people who could break down problems into manageable pieces and then work them through to completion. Their advice to me always was the same—"keep it simple, work hard, and success will take care of itself."

The concepts for succeeding in business are not as grandiose or complicated as some people would have you believe. In some ways, they are quite similar to things you do every day. For example, consider the preparation involved in fixing a Sunday dinner. You first start with an idea of what it is you would like to create. Then you do a quick inventory of the cupboard, assess your time and your family's time to share the meal. You need a strategy for shopping, preparing the meal, and enjoying it.

That's easy enough, you say; you've prepared hundreds of Sunday dinners, but you've never gone into business for yourself. My advice is not to be overwhelmed by the size of the dream or the task. Break problems down into manageable pieces, focus on execution, and keep it simple.

One of the most successful men that I have ever known was my father, G. W. Phelan. As a commercial banker in the 1940s and 1950s in Denver, he was trusted and respected by many in the small business community. In the early years, most of his clients were small business owners who came from all walks of life. On Sundays we would often drive around town, and my father would point out his customers' businesses and describe their origins, struggles, and success. I knew then that I wanted my own business, and so I took in everything he said and tried to find out as much as possible about each owner. I was intrigued by what distinguished a small business owner from one who owned a large business, and by those who succeeded and those who failed. At about the age of ten I was pressing my father for answers to all the questions that seemed important to me at the time, such as, how much money I needed, how much schooling was required, and how old I had to be to get started (the questions haven't changed that much over the years). I didn't have a clue to what business I wanted, just a small business. It was the lifestyle and a chance at independence and wealth that appealed to me. Being the good father, he advised me to stay in school as long as possible, save my money, and to learn to do something well. I had often mentioned having my own shoe-repair shop, one of many ambitions that was lost in childhood. His response was, "learn the trade better than anyone else so that customers know your work and seek you out." He also said that successful business owners from all walks of life shared one thing in common, and that was "intensity." Where the faint of heart will back away from confrontation or disappointing setbacks, the person who succeeds in business, or any other worthwhile undertaking, is persistent and has the ability to focus and complete tasks.

My father once brought home just such a person. His name was Mr. Alfred Kohl, who was a very prosperous businessman and had lived in Germany during the time of

Hitler. As a Jew, he lost everything and was sent to a concentration camp. After the war he fled to America with only his personal belongings, where then in his mid-fifties, he was eager to start again.

My father's bank had made him a small loan, which he used to purchase an old loom in order to begin again in the textile business. In listening to him talk, he would only address the issues at hand and occasionally speculate on the future. Unfortunately, Mr. Kohl died a short time later as a result of the harsh treatment in the concentration camp. But his determination and intensity helped me to appreciate the extraordinary power in the discipline of persistence. He was able to focus on the task at hand and work through each problem, without ever recognizing the prospect of defeat.

Owning your own business can be somewhat of an ego trip. The successful business owners that I have talked with, however, certainly have not demonstrated an excess of bravado. But in an unemotional way they described some of their "setbacks" that would lead me to believe they had some reality checks along the way.

One challenge you will face is overcoming the mistaken notion that when you are in business, you no longer have to work for anyone else. When you own your own business, you must understand that you work for everyone else, that is if you want to be successful. You will never survive with unhappy customers, disgruntled employees, or impatient bankers. You simply have to meet all needs, and more than once you may look back fondly on the structured environment that you left when you only had to please one boss.

Job satisfaction also is a little more difficult to appreciate when you're on your own; at least it will take on a different form. When you work for someone else, the job descriptions and expectations are usually more clear. Therefore, performance could be measured against some standard, and feedback would let you know just how you were doing. At least that's how it is supposed to work in theory.

For a small business owner, the job description is so all-encompassing that usually it requires the total success of the business to provide significant satisfaction. There will always be smaller moments of glory, of course, but you seldom have time for reflection, and rarely will there be someone there to say, "nice job."

Business owners also must be versatile. It's important to gain an understanding of inventory models, marketing strategies, balance sheets, cash flow projections, and other business tools. It's not complicated, but it will require time and attention. Many business owners will tell you this is where a lot of the satisfaction and personal growth come from, that is, in learning. One businesswoman told me that if she had known beforehand all the demands that she would have to deal with, she probably wouldn't have gone into business. But she was quick to add that she was glad that she now had her own business, and that being somewhat ignorant turned out to be a blessing.

So many would-be business owners express anxieties about owning a business. I like to call these people the "what-abouts." "What about workers' compensation, health insurance, withholding tax and unemployment insurance?" they ask. While these issues will need attention and some resolution, they shouldn't become major distractions. Learn to focus on your goal and execute your plan. Once the questions and problems begin to arise, you quickly sort them out, establish a priority, roll up your sleeves, and get on with the job. Much of the risk in failing can be eliminated if you can develop a logical and methodical system of working through problems and adhering to your plan.

After you weigh all of the alternatives and determine that owning your own business is the best way of achieving independence, wealth, and job satisfaction, then embrace the challenge with the conviction that your strength and uniqueness (along with a little good fortune) will carry you through. It won't always be clear to you as you start down the path just what obstacles lie ahead. But you must believe that your best effort will be as good as anyone else's, and you will make more good decisions than bad.

While attending high school, I worked part-time as a bus boy at the very fashionable Cherry Hills Country Club in Denver. One Saturday afternoon, about ten minutes before my scheduled dinner break, the head waiter instructed me to go outside and remove all the umbrellas from the lawn tables and then stack them neatly on the south side of the building. There must have been about twenty tables, and there was no way I could have completed the task in time to have dinner with my friends. But when you are fifteen years old, everything seems possible, and so I began my task. With the wind gusting and my lack of knowledge about dismantling umbrellas, the first table proved to be quite a match. Watching my struggle was a gentleman seated at a corner table, along with about six other men. He rose to his feet and hurried to my assistance. After we had the first umbrella under control, he looked around and asked, "Do you have any more to take down?" I said, "Yes sir, I have to take them all down and then stack them on the south side of the clubhouse." "Well, let's get on with it then," he said, and with a wave of his hand the other men at the table joined us. The chore was completed in about ten minutes, and I was off to dinner with my friends. I later learned that the man who came to my assistance was Dwight Eisenhower! Sometimes, I guess, it's better to be lucky than good.

Your dream must start with confidence. You are not always going to have the answers, and you won't always know how things are going to turn out. But that's part of the excitement of owning your own business.

2

What Business Is Right For Me?

It was 7:30 Monday morning and Jerry Mollica was off to work with a bundle of homemade sausage under his arm. These weren't just "any" sausages—Jerry's grandfather had brought the recipe over from Italy. Making sausage for family and friends at work was a labor of love for Jerry. That his sausages were so well received gave Jerry the idea of going into business for himself. His parents endorsed the idea, the three formed a partnership, and shortly afterward opened the doors of Mollica's Italian Market and Deli.

After six successful years, the Mollicas shared their views on "making it" in the restaurant business. Their key to success does not differ much from other types of business, a common thread that runs through the fabric of those who succeed.

They listed the following ingredients for success: hard work, knowing their product, teamwork, organization, quality, financial control, and finding a niche in the market. In their case, the niche was Italian food with a home-cooked flavor that has served them well in a fickle market.

Selecting the right business is the one obstacle that stops most would-be business owners. It can be a slow and tedious process, and it shouldn't be rushed. When you go into business, do so on your terms and when you feel the time is right. Don't be easily discouraged when things don't fall into place, and don't accept anything less than what meets your goals.

A common mistake is shopping for a business in the same manner as buying a house, by scanning newspaper ads or looking at business broker lists with the thought, "When I see something I like, I'll buy it."

The process for finding the "right" business for those who have been successful is often similar to Jerry Mollica's. He started with a unique perspective, a particular skill, specialized training, or an insight into a need.

How many times have you said, "What this town needs is a good restaurant." That declaration comes from your unique perception, and you will subconsciously envision the type, size, and probable location. Most of us handle these moments of inspiration with fleeting delight and then dismiss them as an idle daydream. To the serious entrepreneur, it may become an action item demanding additional thought.

Working as a volunteer counselor in the SCORE office gave me the opportunity to counsel a young couple who had just moved to the Rocky Mountain area from the West Coast. They had an interest in developing a coffee shop, much like the ones so popular in California. Owning a business would be a new experience for them, but the opportunity to introduce something new to the city and to be a success was something they had to try. Their unique perception started with an awareness, followed by a dream, and then steps toward making the dream a reality.

Finding that right business need not be a search for the unusual. It is not necessary to think in grandiose or revolutionary terms. Successful owners say doing it your way does not necessarily mean being contrary or operating in a fringe area, but rather in applying your perspective and values to running a mainstream business.

You may have some idea for a business and are just looking for the right place and the right time, or something may hit you from out of the blue. Have you ever found yourself driving across the country and wondering why there isn't a service station right about where your gas tank is showing near empty? One of my favorite fantasies is aroused when I pay high prices for poor service from a merchant who needs a dose of competition. For hours I will dream of ways to take business away from him.

Thinking as a customer and applying your values are good ways to assert your own uniqueness. My standards of good price and service not only prompted me to be critical of a particular merchant, but also fueled my imagination on what might be changed to better serve the customers.

Bagel shops have been popping up all over the place as the "in thing" to do. Much of this activity is a result of happy customers moving to areas without bagel shops and seizing the opportunity for a business.

It all can be traced back to your uniqueness and set of values. Since I am not a frequent bagel customer, I am sure that introducing a bagel shop would never occur to me, but to someone with the bagel habit, who understands the product and customers, introducing a bagel shop would be a natural endeavor.

John Peterson was an engineering manager for a California electronics firm. He was intrigued by two recurring thoughts that seemed to haunt him. The first was the need to qualify additional subcontractors to meet the firm's increased demand for printed circuit boards. The second was his desire to operate his own business some day. A light workload meant he was able to devote some time to organizing a business plan for a small printed circuit board business. With the help of his wife they began their small business that turned out to be both successful and profitable. They disclosed the primary reason for their success as hard work, knowing their product, and good planning.

A very small percentage of truly successful business owners start with a totally new concept. Colonel Sanders may have been the first to introduce fried chicken, but not the first in the fast food service. Technological break-throughs may spawn new products and new companies, but quite often the established companies either imitate, use the patents, or buy the business from the start-up companies.

The vast majority of success stories evolve around someone doing a better-than-average job with an already accepted business concept.

What makes being successful in business so easy is that there are so many mentors from whom we can copy and learn. I find it truly amazing to hear of a business that fails. Surely the owners must have lived in a vacuum or perhaps had deliberately set out to destroy their business. Emulating a successful business seems to me a sure way of avoiding such a failure.

The following two examples are typical success stories based upon the ideas of others and then applying the acquired skills. Linda bought an existing business, while George started his business from scratch. In both cases they were able to observe successful performance and then select those features they wanted in their own business.

Linda Doole found herself without a job one day—a blessing in disguise. She had taken a few classes in flower arranging and discovered she had a flair for design and an affinity for the work. She also wanted to own her own business. In discussing her goals with fellow students, she discovered there was a flower shop for sale in an area that had appeal and potential.

Linda first discussed the dream with her husband and other family members to muster the support she knew was needed. She confided in her husband by saying, "what I really am doing is buying myself a secure job." Realizing she had found a business that matched her talent and desire, she approached the owner and through the listing broker was able to buy her dream.

As the sole proprietor for six years, Linda looked back on the experience and shared her views.

The most difficult hurdle for Linda, or anyone purchasing a business, was determining how much the business was actually worth. The real estate broker offered little help. Linda's attorney reviewed the financial statements and concluded the asking price exceeded the market value by approximately $50,000. She was not to be denied, however, and after long negotiations found a middle ground. Determining the value of the inventory and machinery caused most of the problems. "If only I knew then what I know now," she said, "I could walk into any floral shop in this city today and know exactly what it's worth."

Although Linda still works a six-day week, her enthusiasm for her business has not diminished. She attributes her success to hard work, teamwork, and a supportive family.

She offered advice for the beginner: first, take all the management training you can before going into business. Try to buy a business with an established clientele (do not go through a broker unless you have to). Manage your assets and control your costs from day one. And know when to get away from your business to relax and unwind.

After a tour in the military, George Wilson took a training program for operating heavy earth-moving equipment. After the training program, George worked as an equipment operator for a local contractor. This gave him valuable experience in operating different types of machines and the opportunity to learn the business from the ground up (no pun intended).

After a few years he had mastered his skills, saved a little money, and developed a network of acquaintances who would support him in his own business. With the assistance and support of his wife, they began making money from their own earth-moving business almost immediately.

In responding to the questions relating to success, George listed many tips that we have heard from others, such as:

1. Know your business

2. Work hard

3. Produce quality work

4. Treat employees fairly

5. Retain a good accountant

6. Give customers their money's worth

George echoed another common theme when he concurred that succeeding in business is not that difficult. His position was, "Beating the competition is not that big a deal; nobody wants to work hard anymore or take pride in what they do. Just look around you and you'll see a lot of guys cutting corners and not giving the customer his money's worth."

There is a lot to what George had to say. We can often learn from the mistakes of others as well as from those who are successful. It has become more difficult to find a competent mechanic, an honest repairman, a qualified cook, a conscientious merchant, or a quality-minded craftsman. There are far too many complacent business owners with self-serving goals. Store hours are often set for the benefit of the merchant, not the customer. Prices are established to maximize short-term profits rather than establishing long-term customer loyalty. More retail merchants are passing their problems on to the consumer rather than to correct them. For example, prices you pay in most department stores and grocery stores will include losses attributed to theft, damage, or spoilage. You pay for it—but whose problem should it be? So when you observe those in business, learn from their shortcomings as well as their strengths.

In the examples of Linda and George, it should be pointed out that while one purchased an established business and the other started a new business both are successful. As you review your options for going into your own business, there doesn't seem to be a consensus on whether buying an established business or starting from scratch is the best. (Although I certainly talked with more successful owners who had started from scratch.)

In selecting a business to meet your needs, there is unanimous agreement on these points:

1. Know your products

2. Know how to manage your assets

3. Think like a customer

4. Emulate success

5. Apply your values

6. Make use of your unique perspective

For the sake of simplification, consider these three categories for classifying your business interest and see if they help you focus on what might be right for you: Production, Retail, and Service.

Production

Production is generally viewed as the process of converting raw material into a finished product. Production has gone from a collection of small, widely-dispersed, family-owned companies to large, publicly-owned industries. In more recent times there has been some return to the smaller, more flexible companies, which are tied to larger firms through subcontracting relationships. Federal and state workplace and work force regulations make it more expensive for the larger firms to retain high employment in times of economic uncertainty. Hence, these regulations have stimulated some restructuring of large industries in the U.S. At this time, many of these government regulations are less stringent on smaller companies, and the end result has been a modest growth in the number of small to medium-sized firms.

The opportunity to succeed in a small production business is probably as good now as it has been in years. But a local business broker told me that the ratio of qualified buyers looking for profitable production businesses is about ten buyers for every one business for sale. One reason for that statistic is the large number of middle to upper managers who have lost their jobs in corporate America and are now looking to purchase a familiar business. So the opportunity here might be to start a production business, and then place it on the market for sale.

There are four key ingredients to a successful production operation:

1. Controlling quality

2. Controlling cost

3. Product development

4. Marketing

If you are familiar with the production processes, or can team up with a group of partners who can cover all the bases, then you might find a suitable opportunity awaiting you in that small business community.

Several businessmen in this field shared their views on some of the ongoing challenges. Topping the list was finding lucrative contracts with customer firms. Some suggested starting at the bottom by taking small, low-tech work as one way to develop a reputation and establish m relationships. Another common approach was to offer a unique technology the larger firms tend to avoid. But that can require high capitalization costs to provide the service. Ideally, your firm should be diversified so that major shifts in technology will not leave you high and dry with obsolete equipment.

Another challenge mentioned was documentation. Each parent firm has its own format, which means your own in-house control must be flexible to keep up with the various demands. The businessmen queried also had concern for increasing government regulation in the areas of health care, training, family issues, and wages.

Many of us equate a production facility with high-speed lines, putting out hundreds of like-products in a tightly controlled and monitored environment. But this is not always the case. There also is a great deal of activity in the so-called "micro-industrial" arena. I had the good fortune of meeting a middle-aged woman who had converted a bedroom in her home into a very efficient and profitable "hat-production" business. She would purchase raw material in the form of silk, felt, ribbons, and feathers and then fashion them into hats of her own design. She was able to

wholesale everything she could make to two large department stores. Because of the reputation for quality that she
had acquired, she was now considering opening a retail out-
let, while still pursuing more of the wholesale market. Her
reputation for quality, uniqueness, and price had spread to
other major department stores, which were anxious to stock
her products.

She had found a niche that the larger apparel suppliers
viewed as a nuisance market and were not willing to compete. The retailers were delighted to have a local craftsman
who was willing to stock their shelves using "just-in-time"
inventories, with styles popular among the local people.
With her contacts and product acceptance, she strongly
considered adding other accessory lines.

She had started her business by making hats for family
and friends but quickly recognized her skill for both
research and development (R & D) and production. In our
counseling sessions, we worked on cash flow (finance) and
marketing.

There are many success stories like this about people
who go into production on a small but profitable scale.
They define a need by thinking as a customer and then
applying their skills to meet the market demand.

Retail

There are more opportunities in the retail sector than
anywhere else for the small business owner. Success or
failure in this area is really a function of your ability to
work well with people. So often I hear someone who is

thinking about opening a small retail business say, "I like people." "Liking" people has little to do with it. If you are to succeed in this type of business, you must understand, satisfy, work with, and listen to people.

Charles McQueen opened a rather large pet shop in a space that was once occupied by a grocery store. Charles had several things going for him.

1. He graduated from college as a business major

2. His brother owned a pet-supply wholesale business

3. He was a hard worker

4. He had a supportive family

Charles was not someone whom you would classify as personable. But he had a way of relating to everyone in a very nonthreatening, understanding, and caring way. He would spend as much time and would demonstrate the same level of courtesy with a young child spending twenty-seven cents on a box of turtle food as he would with an adult spending hundreds of dollars on an aquarium system. He didn't smile much, nor was he good at small talk or handing out compliments. Yet, people felt comfortable with Charles; he served them well. Did he like people? Well, I never asked, but I suspect his answer might have been, "I like their money."

Another business owner much like Charles was Sam Livingston. Sam dropped out of school when he was quite young and began collecting scrap and junk items he would find in alleys. He could be seen pushing his wagon from early in the morning until late in the evening. He would then haul his treasures to the backyard of his mother's home. He would attempt to sell the better material. Some things he would repair and the remainder was left to accumulate. Before long he had gained a reputation for having a little bit of everything and in time established a network of scrap-collecting friends with whom he would deal. With the outbreak of World War II his scrap metal jumped in value overnight. Seeing an opportunity, he doubled his efforts and bought out some of his friends. Sam watched with delight as his inventory continued to increase in value. He purchased the house next door to his mother and expanded by turning the house into a retail store and filling the backyard with more scrap.

Sam Livingston of Livingston Auto was a very successful businessman. You would always find him in the store, in the backyard with his scrap, or talking with other junk dealers. I watched Sam work with his customers. He had much the same personality as Charles. I don't believe I ever saw him smile, but he was very knowledgeable and could relate well to his customers. Once I heard a customer ask for a particular hubcap that had fallen off his car. Sam responded by saying he would sell him one but he would probably lose it, too. "Poor design," Sam said. "I could make a fortune just selling those hubcaps; better if you would switch to a different type." Sam's interest was in satisfying the needs of his customers, which in turn made his business grow.

Many people in the retail business view it simply as an activity in collecting a transfer fee. You buy a product at wholesale price, mark it up, and then sell it for a profit. Those who are successful, however, know that satisfying customers' needs is what makes the difference. When a customer returns a faulty product, he is not interested in explanations; he wants a good product and wants the retailer to stand behind it.

Retailers whom I have interviewed have offered the following advice:

1. Know your product lines and carry only quality items

2. Understand your profit margins

3. Turn over your inventory every ninety days

4. Never get emotional with a customer (Other customers watch how you treat people)

5. Be willing to make concessions when you feel a customer has been wronged

Opening a retail business is quite exciting and can offer the owner opportunities for diversification and personal growth. Successful owners are involved in dealing with vendors, marketing products, inventory management, pricing, financial management, and sales.

The major advantage in selecting the retail field is the transferability of skills. One who succeeds in a haberdasher's shop in Vermont probably would do well opening such a shop in California, or even a retail store with a totally different product line.

A successful clothing store owner sold his business and with the profits opened a large discount liquor store. His explanation was, "people spend more money on liquor than they do on clothes." He was able to transfer to a new product line effortlessly as far as his business skills were concerned. From the opening day the business showed a profit because of his management skills and his ability to meet customer needs.

Service

The service sector has experienced explosive growth in the past ten years. Computer technology, particularly in wide area networking such as Internet, and the phenomenal growth of fax transmissions, has opened up the communication highway to almost everyone. Product and sales representatives now can serve a larger customer base without leaving their offices. Desk-top publishers are picking up lucrative advertising contracts from such giants as the phone companies.

Recently, I counseled a young businesswoman who owned and operated a phone-answering service. Most of her customers were doctors who were delighted with the twenty-four hour service that she offered.

Another businesswoman was doing quite well at writing résumés for college graduates and others seeking employment. She was able to work out of her home at hours convenient to her family.

We used to think of the service industry as maid and janitorial services, cleaners, or car washes. These businesses still are flourishing, but so many new concepts have hit the market that the term "service" needs to be redefined.

To begin thinking about service areas, start with the ideas of what people do not like to do themselves or are unable to do. Begin with yourself. What tasks do you find annoying or time consuming? Here are a few of mine:

1. Grocery shopping

2. House cleaning

3. Remembering birthdays and anniversaries

4. Washing the car

5. Maintaining the yard

6. Standing in line for tickets

7. Preparing taxes

8. Shopping for a car

9. Doing home repairs

After examining your own personal dislikes, consider those of others. The elderly, for example, find it difficult to meet appointments or do shopping in inclement weather; they always seem to have need for a fence or a back door repair.

Reliable and reasonable day care centers always are in demand. With the aging population, there is an increasing demand for nursing homes as well as "parent-sitters" who will look in on the seniors while the juniors are out of town.

House-sitting and plant-sitting often provide college students with a chance to make an extra dollar. Travel agencies are diversifying into the tour guide business by offering local or national tours, either independently or in concert with other agencies.

My oldest daughter, Monica Katsos, opened her own plantscape business for residential and commercial customers. She had a knowledge of plants and shrubs along with a flair for design and was able to start a business with a minimum amount of capital. As business increased, she hired people to help with the physical aspects of the work, freeing her to focus on marketing and cash flow projections. Yard maintenance, while quite lucrative, can be very seasonal in some areas, but generally there is some year-round demand for those willing to go after it.

The most appealing reason for entering the service sector is the low capital requirement. This turns out to be a double-edged sword, however, as it invites competition. Those who are tenacious and succeed are normally people with personal charisma who are willing to work hard at customer satisfaction.

If this field is of interest to you, start by identifying a customer need. As a customer, you already may have an insight. Do not be discouraged if someone else already offers that service. Find out all you can about the competition and what they offer. Talk with potential customers to learn about their exact needs; then start small enough to gain a foothold. If you do your job well, your reputation will spread faster than you can imagine, and growth and profit will follow. If you do poorly, that reputation also will spread equally as fast. Your good name and reputation for quality and fair prices will be the deciding factor in your success.

One of the major problems in the service industry is pricing. It is quite easy to get established by undercutting the competition; but this method of "low-balling" could come back to haunt you. Your pricing structure should be based on these cost factors: Labor, Material, and Overhead.

When estimating a job, or when billing a customer, separate the various labor charges whenever possible. For example, in the landscape business, the design and layout of a particular job might command a wage rate higher than the planting and watering of trees. But some merchants, in an attempt to simplify pricing, will try to come up with an average rate based on some volume weighted technique. While that may make your bookkeeping easier, it may be disturbing to a customer who sees a $20 per hour labor charge when all they notice is someone watering the trees occasionally.

When your service includes materials, those costs should be passed on to the customer. Attorneys pass on the cost of paper when copying documents, a masseur or masseuse passes on the cost of oils and creams, and the landscaper charges for the cost of trees and shrubs. If you purchase your materials at wholesale prices, you are certainly entitled to a fair markup, but if you buy the material at retail and add some markup, it is questionable if you are serving your customer fairly.

Many states require sales tax collection on every retail sale; for this you will need a city, county, and perhaps a state sales tax license. Any taxes collected must then be paid (usually monthly) to the taxing entity. Your government agencies will be more than happy to answer your questions and assist you in getting started.

Overhead is the one area that needs the most attention if you are to be thorough in your pricing. Overhead charges include such things as:

1. Utilities

2. Office expenses

3. Bookkeeping and tax preparation

4. Rent or lease payments

5. Insurance premiums

The temptation is to throw everything questionable into overhead. If your pricing is to be competitive and you are to be profitable, then allocate every cost you can. For example, the cost of gasoline for your trucks to run back and forth to a construction site should be a direct charge to the project being serviced, and not simply paid monthly and dispersed as an overhead charge. On the other hand, rent on your building, or insurance premiums, might be more difficult to assign to any specific job, so you would be justified in collecting these costs, and then passing them on to all of your customers on a percentage basis. For example, you may calculate your overhead rate to be 10 percent, based on all of your overhead costs. You could then burden either labor or material as a means of passing these costs on to your customers. For example, if you were in the retail business, you would increase the cost of your products by 10 percent to cover your overhead expenses. Your accountant can help you identify the appropriate overhead charges and calculate the proper rate.

After you structure your pricing, based on the accurate assessment of your costs, compare your prices with others. If you find it difficult to compete on price, then consider offering something the competition doesn't have, such as service. Don't begin cutting your prices for market share if you want to remain in business. Selling for less, to be competitive, is a sure recipe for disaster.

You may also want to factor a profit margin into the overhead rate by raising the multiple to a level that will produce your targeted return on investment. If your goal is to generate a 15 percent profit level, and all of your revenue comes from the sale of material, then price your products high enough to produce that return. This is how you burden material with the overhead charges. Now, if your business is in the service sector, and most of your income is derived from labor charges, then you would burden labor with the overhead charges. One merchant told me that he would take his wholesale cost and multiply by three to arrive at a selling price. Whatever multiple you use, remember to price your products or service at a level that covers all of your costs, including the cost of money. This method gives you a bench mark, where you now know how much you must charge, to at least break even or show a profit. If the market will allow higher prices, then you have a pleasant problem to consider. If, however, the market demands lower prices, then you have a more difficult problem. Incidentally, this exercise is better served if you do it before going into business, as part of the market analysis, and not after you discover you're losing money. Your banker or accountant can help with some of the calculations, and you should be prepared to estimate volume levels, which is a key factor in any pricing strategy.

Arts and Crafts

In addition to production, retail, and service there is a fourth category that will often encompass all three, and that is the world of arts and crafts.

In Albuquerque, New Mexico, I happened upon one of the Gallagher Galleries in Old Town. Pat Gallagher is an artisan/businessman with the talent for fashioning figures out of metal with a turquoise lamination. Though much of his work is similar, each piece has unique and original features. Pat Gallagher has three galleries in Old Town and one in Scottsdale, Arizona. The Gallagher Galleries also feature Southwest art from a number of different artists.

The numerous craft shows, outlets, and galleries across the country offer artists an opportunity to market their work without starting a business. Yet for ambitious artists, who want to expand both financially and artistically, owning their own business offers a solution.

Michael Garman is a western artist who enjoys sculpturing western life in the early 1900s. To show his pieces in their natural setting, he constructed numerous "old city" backgrounds, in miniature scale, and opened a very impressive gallery for public viewing. People now pay, for not only his art, but to walk through several of his showrooms.

Ray Swanson, a very prominent southwestern artist, has developed such a following that people literally stand in line for his works. After years of moving his pieces from gallery to gallery across the country, Ray now sends most of his work to a gallery owned by his daughter and son-in-law. In talking with him, you get the feeling that he is anything but a temperamental artist, but rather a very shrewd businessman.

Determining which business is best for you may be something that comes with time. Your first attempt may be exactly what you have always wanted, or it may be the first step that will lead to your ultimate business. I have yet to talk to a successful business person who didn't change or evolve their business over time.

Starting with your own values and perceptions, thinking as a customer, looking for needs or opportunities, and then emulating success is certainly a proven approach to launching a successful career in the small business community.

By considering production, retail, service, or self-expression (artist), you will have taken a major step in identifying your interest.

3

Selecting a Business Platform

Every entrepreneur harbors various degrees of tolerance for risk. Although I would not characterize any successful business owner as a "risk-taker," some are certainly more conservative than others. The whole notion of risk is often a paramount concern to those starting a business for the first time. Many will view risk as the crucial determining factor in selecting a starting platform for a business. The platforms available are really the following three—although there can be several variations or combinations.

1. Start your own business

2. Buy an existing business

3. Buy a franchise

Many who are thinking of their own business for the first time will weigh the pros and cons of each choice, factor in their own risk threshold, and then embark on some selection process.

Interestingly enough, when talking with successful business owners, few had followed this approach. They admitted to being aware of the difference between starting and buying a business, and they conceded that buying a business or a franchise gave the appearance of being less risky. However, they did not believe that to always be the case. They felt that buying an established business or opening a franchise could be very risky.

In our conversations, the successful business owners seemed to take exception with the emphasis on considering risk. One very successful owner explained, "risk is something gamblers take, not business owners."

A prominent woman in the field of real estate pointed out that a great many people who could ill-afford to lose money often will gamble. "Better to spend the limited resources on education or a book on budgeting," she said. In her early business years she said that taking any risk was unconscionable, and that being frugal and deliberate was the order of the day. Now, with some affluence, she does not mind taking some chances—"I can afford it now, but I still will not take a chance unless the odds are in my favor."

Successful business owners believe that selecting a business platform should be the product of a carefully developed plan. Considering the pros and cons of various platforms and then making a selection from a broker's list, a newspaper ad, or a franchise publication is precisely what they thought should not be done.

Starting a Business

The majority of successful business owners interviewed had started their own businesses. A few had purchased a "shell" and then added resources for expansion. I was somewhat surprised to find that so many had started from scratch. The U.S. Department of Commerce produces data suggesting that 85 percent of start-up businesses will fail in the first ten years. Could it be that I was talking with the 15 percent who succeeded, or could it be there is something wrong with the data? I suspect that a business failure within ten years is one that has been sold and resold a number of times. It was probably ill-defined from the beginning and drained several owners of their money.

If you are going to fail at something, it should certainly not take you ten years to accomplish it. A business that is not on its feet in six months will probably never walk, much less run. Bill Frazier, who founded Frazier Electric Supply, has opened several businesses in his illustrious career and each realized a profit within two months. Is that unusual? Bill thinks it should be the norm, if you know what you are doing.

A middle-aged couple related their struggle in keeping a liquor store afloat. The wife worked the business full time while her husband held down a well-paying job with another employer. The liquor store was losing $1,000 a month. Fortunately the husband's income could cover the loss. This had been going on for some time, and with additional hard work, I suppose they could stretch this operation out for ten years to qualify as an average loser.

Once again we see the importance of developing goals and plans, conducting a market analysis, and understanding pricing concepts before going into business.

People who start their own business from scratch usually do so for one of the following reasons:

1. They have a special niche that no other business offers

2. There is a desirable location for a business where none exists

3. There is a personal preference to start very small (hobby approach)

4. They have limited capital or time

5. They have a highly specialized one-person business such as doctor, attorney, consultant, etc.

What are the major challenges in starting a business from scratch? Those who have succeeded in starting their own business agree that marketing, or name-recognition, usually demands an inordinate amount of time at the beginning. Winning customers from the competition or introducing a new service or product will require a sound marketing plan and time.

As part of the overall business plan, the marketing section should begin with a market analysis. How big is the total pie from which you intend to take a piece? If you had the whole pie, would it be large enough to satisfy your hunger? When you thoroughly understand the composition of the pie, then you can begin to focus on a marketing strategy.

A market strategy is a detailed plan of how you are going to get this pie onto your plate. Start by developing a profile of your customer's habits, social tastes, etc. Equipped with this knowledge, you will better understand where and how to advertise and how to present your product or service at the right price.

Another hurdle that a new business faces is recruiting reliable vendors. It is not difficult to find sales representatives or distributors who seem willing to wholesale; to find reliable ones is more difficult. I visited a gift shop whose business had tripled in five years. The owner pointed out that she now had more than 2,500 different items in the shop. Some of her earlier suppliers had tried not only to unload dead stock on her but to insist on higher inventory levels than were necessary.

What made her successful was the same thing I have heard over and over. Know your business! In this particular case, the owner had worked in several gift shops prior to opening her own. She understood her customers, the market trends, stock levels, turnover rates, and common purchase terms. No slick salesperson would be able to sell her any boat anchors.

Pricing the product or service can be difficult in some markets. When you consider that some markets allow for only 1.5 percent profit margin before taxes, you can appreciate the need for understanding cost and pricing. Selling prices, discounts, and terms should be calculated rather than set arbitrarily. It is easy to fall victim to the concept of "whatever the market will bear," or "whatever the competition is doing." As we discussed earlier, pricing should be based on cost, volume, and a predetermined return on investment. Your pricing policy will be an important element of the marketing strategy. You may discover there are markets that you cannot afford to be in and products or services you cannot afford to offer. Determine this before, not after you are in business.

Many other issues in opening a new business are quite mechanical and, while very important, are not always considered major hurdles. For example:

Registering your business name

To protect yourself from selecting a name already in use and preventing anyone else from using your name, you need to register the trade name of your business. The local office of the State Department of Revenue can do this for you in a matter of minutes, for a nominal fee. If your business is to be incorporated, you may be directed to the offices of the Secretary of State. In either case, start with your Department of Revenue.

You may also find that the local bankers will ask for proof of this registration before opening a business account in that name.

Selecting a legal entity

Most small businesses start as a sole proprietorship, or a partnership, because it's cheap and simple. And in many cases it works out just fine. If you ever decide to incorporate, you may find that your business name will have to be changed. So before going for the cheap and simple, spend some time with an attorney and discuss your options. Many married couples, who form partnerships, never take the time to file a partnership agreement, relying instead on marriage laws and the rights of survival. The best advice is to check the laws in your state with a competent attorney.

Acquiring licenses

The type of license(s) required of your business can certainly vary from one location to another. California may not require a vendor license for a lemonade stand, but Texas might. Rather than ask the uninformed, contact either your local City Clerk, or the State Department of Revenue for compliance information. In addition, inquire into zoning regulations to ensure your business is located properly.

The State and Federal Departments of Revenue will assist you with sales tax, income tax, and employment tax forms and registration. As you make the rounds from one agency to another, you will find most of the people very helpful and willing to give a helping hand.

Setting up books

Unless you have experience in bookkeeping or someone to help you, locate a good accountant to assist you in setting up your business books! Even if you have a computer and a good software package, talk with an accountant. Business books really serve two purposes: first, all of the taxing agencies that you serve have definite requirements you must meet, and second, and most important, your books will help you manage your business. Keep records that serve your needs, and meet the requirements of the various government offices.

For purposes of growth, expansion, and diversification, several larger, more successful business owners found it advantageous to buy out competitors or other businesses similar to their own. Some owners have revealed that their success was only vaguely related to their original start-up business concept. As time passed, they had discovered other opportunities, and rather than integrate through acquisition, they leapfrogged into something different. For example: one retail grocer ended up being more successful as a wholesale distributor.

Buying a Business

The easiest way to become an overnight business owner is to buy an existing business. The big advantage is acquiring an established cash flow. There are certainly some other advantages worth mentioning.

Let us assume that your goal was to own a family restaurant. Your business plan described precisely what the size would be, the location, and the type of food you would offer. In doing the start-up cost analysis, you were able to place a value on chairs, tables, cooking range, refrigerators, counter tops and other fixtures. A restaurant came on the market with many of the things you wanted except for the location and menu. The opportunity might prompt you to buy the assets at a market discount and move everything to a location of your choice.

In this case you would not be paying for good will, a business name, or noncompete compensation. If it were a distressed sale or bankruptcy, however, you might find an opportunity to reduce your start-up cost by purchasing assets at a discount.

Another advantage of buying an established business is that many of the start-up problems have been factored out including "name-recognition." As the new owner, you can focus your energies on improvements, expansions, and optimizing profit.

Remember that three key elements for succeeding in business will be your ability to raise capital, manage your assets, and deal with personnel issues. When you buy a business, there is an opportunity to resolve two of these elements. If you can obtain owner-financing at a reasonable rate, you will have gone a long way toward raising capital. If the current staff is willing to stay with the business (at your pleasure, of course), you will have added a dimension of stability and continuity that may prove valuable.

There are, of course, some drawbacks to buying a business. The challenge is to get the business at a fair market price or less. One business owner told me that every owner has a price at which he or she would sell the business. If you offer a successful owner a purchase price that is "fair," he probably would not sell. If you offered 1.5 to 2 times what the business was worth, he might sell.

Conversely, if you offer an unsuccessful owner a purchase price that is fair, they would probably sell. The better offer would be 0.5 to .75 of what the business is worth.

Getting an objective appraisal of the worth of a business can be difficult. In Chapter 5 we will discuss various methods. One of the interesting views that successful business owners shared with me was their ability to value other similar types of businesses. For example, the restaurant owner, the florist, and the small manufacturing firm all agreed they could walk through a business similar to theirs and tell you within a few thousand dollars what the business is worth. An owner of a small printing firm told me that she could look at the presses and their invoices of paper purchases and tell what the market value of the business should be.

There is no substitute for knowing the business. Recently, a middle manager from corporate America asked my advice on purchasing a small machine shop. He had just lost a good job and at age fifty-seven wanted to find a small business to finish out his working years. In reviewing the assets and past earnings of this shop, a market value of between $60,000 and $70,000 seemed reasonable to me. The owner was asking $375,000 for the business. What was more frightening was that the potential buyer was looking for ways to raise the money to buy the business.

His pension plan, 401K, and personal savings amounted to about $275,000, and he was seeking advice on raising the balance. His experience in this type of business was absolutely zero. The seller had him convinced that only half of the earnings had ever been reported, and therefore the business was worth considerably more than the book value.

This story is more common than you can imagine. The real estate broker, who provided the listing, was acting as an agent for the seller and offered little support to the buyer. Could the buyer sue for misrepresentation or fraud if he later found that the earnings were less than claimed? Perhaps! Establishing guilt would be difficult, and legal fees might prove to be very expensive.

Better to know the business beforehand or seek the counsel and opinion of others who may be familiar with the type of business you are considering. There is an abundance of free counsel available. Check your phone book for these two agencies:

- Service Corps of Retired Executives (SCORE)

- Small Business Development Center (SBDC)

Another great source is other business owners. You will find most small business owners are very willing to discuss most aspects of their business with those seeking advice, though most are very busy, and it might be difficult to catch them when they have time.

The Phelan family purchased an existing greenhouse business as a starting point for their first venture. After two years they were able to buy acreage in another part of the city where, one year later, they opened a new greenhouse business under a different name. The original business would fall under the category of "buying a business," while their second location was a "start-up."

This is a very common method for expansion. The interesting phenomenon in the last example was the deliberate attempt to decouple the operations. There was no sharing of customers, name recognition, equipment, or purchasing agreements. However, the second operation, which became an overnight success and generated profit immediately, did benefit from experienced managers who moved over from the original greenhouse business.

The message here is twofold:

1. Buying an existing business is an easy way to get started

2. If you know what you are doing, a start-up business can be profitable from day one

Buying a Franchise

According to the International Franchise Association, located in Washington, D.C., a new franchise opens somewhere in the United States every sixteen minutes—and the franchised businesses now employ 7.2 million people. John Naisbitt, author of *Megatrends* and *Megatrends 2000*, has been quoted as saying, "Franchising is the most successful marketing concept ever created."

The franchise can be a very attractive option. Many entrepreneurs are turning to the franchise as a way of reducing risk and generating instant profit. The franchise has appeal because of high success rates and a host of support features. Most franchise organizations will offer support in the following areas:

1. Product and management training

2. Financial assistance

3. Organizational directions

4. Local and national marketing support

The price range and conditions for buying a franchise vary from one business to another. If you wish to purchase a Burger King restaurant, for instance, you would need a net worth of $500,000 of which $200,000 must be in cash or liquid assets (*Franklin Opportunities Handbook, 1994*). This amount assumes that you would develop the land and construct the building. For markets where the land and building would be developed by Burger King and leased to the franchisee, a net worth of $170,000 must be in cash or liquid assets.

Franchise fees for Dunkin Donuts of America, Inc., range from $27,000 to $40,000 depending on the geograph- ical area and whether the franchise owns or controls the real estate. Working capital is approximately $18,000.

Investing in a proven business and getting the managerial and product support can be very beneficial. It is not unusual for a successful franchisee to buy additional units as a method of expansion. I found a business person in a large city who owned six McDonald franchises. A large family in a smaller city owned three Dunkin Donut franchises.

Before taking the plunge into the franchise waters, however, there are a number of steps you should take. Review once again your reasons for going into business. What is your ultimate goal, where do you want to go, and what plans have you formulated to get there? If you first select a franchise and then develop a business plan, which somehow helps you describe a goal, you have managed to work the process backwards. It is like starting with the answer and then trying to think up a good question.

Is independence one of your goals? Are you tired of working for someone else? Owning a franchise may not be for you. Depending on the franchise, levels of dependence will vary. You may have a contractual obligation to purchase your material from the parent company even if you can buy better quality at a lower price somewhere else. You may find yourself making monthly payments to the franchiser in support of national advertising that does not seem to benefit you directly.

Begin by talking with others who own a franchise. Have them describe for you the pros and cons of that particular franchise. If you are negotiating to purchase an existing franchise, have an accountant review the earning statements and tax returns. If you're interested in buying a new franchise, involve your accountant in reviewing their revenue and cost projections, along with their assumptions.

Insist that your attorney be allowed to review all of the contract agreements for not only getting into business—but also for getting out, or renewing the franchise. States will vary on their disclosure laws, so it is very important that you select a local attorney who is familiar with franchise contracts. The large reputable franchises are just as anxious for you to succeed as you are; you will find them very cooperative and willing to work with your team. Any franchiser who acts differently is one to avoid.

Cottage Industries

There is an increasing number of people who have an interest in working out of their homes. The increase in the number of working, single parents has increased the demand for home-operated businesses, and more people have started some very profitable businesses. Examples of these types of businesses are:

1. Day care centers

2. Desk top publishing

3. Software firms

4. Telemarketing

5. Bed and breakfasts

6. Writing books and articles

7. Light manufacturing

8. Small repair shops

9. Arts and crafts

With the communications highway becoming more accessible, the use of phones, fax machines, computers, and even the television, expand the potential for working at home.

In this home environment people can satisfy many of their goals of independence, wealth, and a sense of contribution. The start-up capital for such a business often is quite nominal. There are, of course, some restrictions that you should understand and evaluate before going down this road.

Proper zoning is often a hurdle that must be resolved before you alienate not only your city but also your neighbors. If you sell any product, you will be required to have a city and state sales tax license; you may be confronted by the zoning board at this stage of the process or they may "find you out" when you register your business name. Such a registration with the Department of Revenue will protect you against someone else using your name and also will legitimize profit and loss claims you will want to make on your income tax.

Though many cottage businesses function without being in compliance with local zoning laws, all it takes to shut you down is one phone call from an irate neighbor or customer. Excuses such as: "I have been doing this for years," or "how about Joe's place across town" will fall on deaf ears. A hassle over proper zoning should be avoided by proper investigation beforehand. You will find your city willing to assist and advise you in this area.

Another consideration in starting a cottage business is the expansion possibility. Few who are just starting a business feel that growth is a major concern. Those who are successful, however, will have to deal with some difficult expansion problems later on.

I talked to a group of successful business owners one evening about the question of growth. A number of them said they were not particularly happy with being "larger." Being small held many fond memories such as, having total control, knowing all aspects of the business, having a minimal number of employees, and being able to spend more time on the machines and with the customers.

They conceded that profit and earnings determined growth more than anything else. Alternative investments were never as attractive as their own business, and, consequently, growth became a product of their own success.

If your cottage business does well, you may have to consider the ramifications of a different location and hiring additional people. The obvious choice, of course, is not to grow but to remain small. But this may prove to be more difficult than you think.

A number of very large successful businesses were started on a very modest scale. Bill Hewlett and Dave Packard founded the Hewlett Packard Co. in Packard's one-car garage. They used Mrs. Packard's kitchen stove to bake the enamel on the instruments' front panels. Today they are a Fortune 500 company. In fact, most of our industrial giants had very modest beginnings.

Many inventions today are developed in basements and garages, and then either sold to corporate America or used as the foundation for a new company. This is cottage industry at its best.

Some of our finest writers and artists do their creative work in the quiet of a home studio rather than a structured office environment.

Interesting hobbies often become profitable businesses. The owner and founder of Axel's Rocks and Stamps, which is now a complete rock store selling lapidary equipment and supplies, started as Mr. Axel's hobby when he worked in corporate America. There he would stop a person in the hallway and proudly exhibit a stone that he had spent much of the night polishing.

Service-oriented businesses are increasingly moving into home locations. Just to mention a few:

- Tax service

- General bookkeeping

- Consulting

- Manufacturing sales representative

- Home cleaning

- Real estate

A general question when selecting a cottage industry is whether to have customers come to you. Such an arrangement means traffic and parking, signs and a storefront, all of which necessitate proper zoning. If you can go to your customer and there is no need for parking vehicles at your home, then you will likely qualify as a cottage business.

The major attractions for this type of business are a relatively small start-up capital, good profit margin, and the comfort of a home environment. Whichever platform you select for going into business, you should begin by determining your goals, developing a plan for achieving those goals, and then selecting the appropriate platform (in that order).

Special Concerns When Buying a Business

Generally, when a person buys a business, he or she is interested in buying future earnings and profit. If a business cannot produce enough earnings to support salaries and some annual profit margin, it usually can be dismissed as a poor investment. Unfortunately, there are far too many cases of people hanging onto a business that produces a meager salary and little or no profit.

Two important things to consider before buying into a business are: will the present earnings pay my salary for work I perform, and will there be enough money left over after expenses to show a profit?

In later chapters we will discuss the profit issue in more detail, but for now suffice it to say that without profit you have just bought yourself a job! Profits can be taken out of the business, or retained for expanding inventories, or other capital investments. Profits, whether withdrawn or retained, are necessary for the continued health of the business. Merely buying a job is a very expensive and short-lived method of gaining independence.

An exception to this would be when real estate or some other tangible asset is included in the business and can appreciate in value over time. For example, buying a car wash that includes land located on a corner lot of a busy street, could offer the opportunity for land appreciation. If working the car wash just pays the owner's wage and the business shows no profit, it still could be viewed as a good investment. The increased valuation of the property is steadily increasing the owner's equity and therefore represents a form of retained earnings.

Buying a job is neither good nor bad from the standpoint of meeting your goals. From an investment standpoint, however, it is not considered very astute.

There are seasoned managers and investors who look for good businesses as investment opportunities. Venture capitalists, who normally track the high tech industries, seek opportunities to invest their money in a game of high risk and high return.

Successful business owners may sell a profitable business and then wait for the opportunity to buy another similar business. Their background and previous experiences allow them to generate short-term profits, sometimes at the expense of long-term gains, and then sell the business. It is for this reason that these two questions be answered when you are purchasing a business.

1. How long has the business been owned?

2. Why is the business being sold?

A savvy business person will carefully examine the business records to highlight the financial health of the investment. If you can buy a business or franchise and then hire someone to run it for you at a profit, you have essentially become a venture capitalist. It is much the same as buying rental property except the risk is greater; hence the return should be greater. Investing in a business just for the pure investment play can be profitable for the experienced and knowledgeable entrepreneur.

In this same vein there are investors and managers who await the business failures. Buying into these opportunities at a fraction of their value and turning the business around for income or sale can be quite lucrative. These types of investors normally network with attorneys and bankers who deal in bankruptcy and foreclosure. Before a case goes into bankruptcy or foreclosure, the creditors may be willing to settle for a fraction of the cost rather than face total loss.

Again, it boils down to knowing your business. These types of managers and investors have learned the techniques for spotting opportunities and then fixing the problems. I was recently told of a young Harvard MBA (age 37) who, after owning two businesses, had paper assets of more than $10 million. I suspect he knew what he is doing!

On the other hand, when you are buying a business that you intend to operate on a long-term basis, understand the history of the business ownership. What you do not want is a business that has been made to look good in order to attract gullible buyers.

4

How Do I Start?

In an earlier example, going into business was compared to fixing a dinner. Before you make any decision requiring action, you must first determine "where you are." Taking stock or inventory of one's assets, both personal and financial, is a fundamental prerequisite for developing a meaningful plan.

Many studies have been conducted over the years to identify traits or behaviors that might serve as indicators of success in small business. Although nothing emerges that would categorically predict success or failure in a business undertaking, it appears that certain of the following characteristics relate to successful entrepreneurs:

- Persistence: Displays goal-oriented behavior and is not easily deterred

- Seeks Information: Continually searches for new information which relates to the business

- Profit oriented: Accepts the notion that profit is a valid measure of success

- Networks: Forms alliances which are helpful for business

- Takes Risks: Takes calculated chances, none less than 50/50 (is not a gambler)

- Achievement Oriented: Behavior is usually in the direction of goal achievement

- Versatility: The ability to deal with a wide variety of people

- Solves Problems: Removes problems by attacking causes as opposed to treating symptoms

- Has Mature Self-Concepts: Realistically knows capabilities and limitations and is comfortable with that

- Works Hard: Spends many hours on business-related things every day

- Handles Multiple Stimuli: When faced with confusing and complex situations, can sort them out and deal with each

- Possesses Vision: Has a vision and is in continuous motion toward its realization

You should be able to identify with most, if not all, of these characteristics. Each type of business has unique demands, but if you do not measure up to these general expectations, it would be wise to consider some other endeavor. The only shame associated with arriving at this conclusion is ignoring the early warning and proceeding with the wrong career choice.

Periodically, we should all subject ourselves to a reality check of some sort. The following questions were developed to help us accomplish just that. Take a moment and answer yes (Y) or no (N) to the following:

1. Do I often engage in independent or contrary thinking?

2. Is leisure time a basic requirement?

3. Do I handle criticism constructively?

4. Do I view managing details as nonproductive?

5. Do I complete most things that I start?

6. Is making money my primary motivation in my career?

7. Do I deal with multiple stimuli?

8. Do I enjoy building consensus?

9. Do I insist on being organized?

10. Does bureaucracy stifle me?

11. Am I tenacious in nature?

12. Are my physical or emotional limitations an issue?

13. Do I seek help when I am in a jam?

14. Must I always have my own way?

15. Are my family and friends supportive?

16. Do I view myself as being flexible?

17. Do I clearly understand my goals?

18. Do I prefer being an individual contributor to managing people?

19. Do I usually work harder than those around me?

20. Am I a perfectionist in every sense?

There is no right or wrong answer to any question—no passing or failing grade. Most business-oriented people will answer the odd-numbered questions in the affirmative and the even-numbered questions with a no. To remove bias, give a copy of these questions to two people who know you well and see how they score you.

Selecting a business that totally matches your attributes is desirable but not always mandatory. For example, if you're buying a machine shop—you might be a great machinist, but have a real distaste for record keeping or dealing with people. The important issue is to identify those areas where you may need to enlist some support or improve your own skills. The bottom line is to know yourself and then search to find the line of business that best fits you.

Next, conduct a financial inventory of your assets. Most businesses that fail do so because they were poorly managed or were under-capitalized, or both.

One of the first decisions you may have to make is how much you should invest and how much money you should keep in reserve. Begin by listing all of your funds that could be converted into cash in less than thirty days. These assets are defined as liquid and would typically include:

Market Value

Cash

Stocks

Bonds

Certificates of Deposit

Money Market Accounts

Other

_____

Total

Stocks and bonds may not be liquid if the market is depressed and cashing them out would result in a loss. If you believe the market is about to rise, you may not feel comfortable selling at this time.

Next, list those sources of funds that might be used to raise additional cash for working capital, expansion capital, or just hard-times capital. Refer to these as your "line of credit" and include among them:

1.　Equity in your home (banks will loan up to 75% of your equity)

2.　Insurance policies (insurance companies will lend up to 60-70% of the cash value of some policies)

3.　Credit cards

4.　Friends/relatives who would loan you money

5.　Lending Institutions (banks and credit unions often will make personal loans to people with good credit ratings)

In addition to these commonly recognized assets, banks will be interested in your current job, your partner or your spouse's job, and any patents, copyrights, or specialized training you may have.

My first experience at owning a business was a music and television repair shop called "Young Records." My partner and brother-in-law shared the daytime duties with me, and we both worked night shift jobs in corporate

America. That neither of us drew a wage from the business in the formative months was an asset as far as the business cash flow was concerned.

Banks commonly refer to the five "C's" when considering a loan application:

- Cash

- Collateral

- Character

- Credit

- Capacity

Capacity refers to the ability of the owners to meet their debt obligations. If there is income generated outside the business (owner's spouse working another job), the bank will view that as personal collateral. Good credit ratings and character references still carry considerable weight with most banks. Therefore do not hesitate to list these as assets.

When our family went into the greenhouse business, my wife managed the entire operation while I remained employed elsewhere. My income helped us qualify for loans and other lines of credit, while my wife used her horticultural and managerial skills to expand the business.

After you have completed the personal and financial inventory, you are ready to set the parameters of your goal.

Your financial assets will help determine the size of the undertaking. Recall the young couple who settled for the four-plex instead of the motel? Buying what they could afford was a prudent decision.

When you purchased your first home, you may have been advised to "stretch" or buy a house just barely within your means. The underlying theory was that your wages would gradually increase, the house payments would remain constant, and inflation would increase the value of the home.

The reverse may be true when buying a business. You will be tempted to retain more earnings for business expansion, and the tradeoff may be your own wage. Also, business expenses are never constant and normally rise, and increases in the value of your business are the result of increased earning and equity, not just inflation.

Bernard Baruch, a successful financier and presidential adviser, claimed that personal funds fall into three categories:

   A—Capital needed to meet the bare essentials, such as rent, food and health

   B—Capital needed to make life more bearable, such as movies, television, and education

   C—Capital used for investment and gain, such as buying stocks, bonds, or buying a business

It would be a mistake to use or pledge any assets that might jeopardize either category A or B when going into business.

A solid business plan, combined with a mindset that equates risks with gamblers, certainly could make the difference between success and failure. Defining your limitations, both personal and financial, should be an integral part of the plan.

The following example may provide you with some insight into how much of your assets you should commit for purchasing or starting a new business and a line of credit or reserve capital for operations. You can leverage your investment (equity) with a debt load of about 3 to 1.

Example #1

	Debt	Equity
Purchase price (PP) $50,000	$37,500	$12,500
Working capital:		
Existing business (5% of PP)		$2,500
Start-up business (20% of PP)		$10,000
Required investment for existing business		$15,000
Required investment for start-up business		$22,500

In example #1, the buyer is looking at a business with a total purchase price (PP) of $50,000. Assuming that the buyer could find a lender willing to lend 70 percent to 80 percent of the purchase price ($37,500), the buyer would have to invest $12,500 of his own money. The ratio between the borrowed amount of $37,500 (debt) and the buyer's money of $12,500 (equity) is 3 to 1, which is the relationship that lending institutions like to see.

Sellers who agree to finance often will offer the same terms, but typically they look for something closer to 50 percent of the buyer's money as a down payment.

If the buyer is purchasing an established business with a positive cash flow, he should set up a cash reserve for working capital no less than 5 percent of the purchase price (PP). In this example, that would be $50,000 multiplied by 5 percent or $2,500. So the total amount of money that the buyer needs to purchase an existing business selling for $50,000 is: $12,500 + $2,500 or $15,000.

If the entrepreneur starts a new business with tangible assets equal to $50,000, he should have a working capital reserve of no less that 20 percent of the start-up cost, which is $50,000 times 20 percent or $10,000. In this case the owner should be prepared to invest $22,000 ($12,500 + $10,000) of his own money.

Example #2

	Debt	Equity
Purchase Price (PP) $100,000	$75,000	$25,000
Working capital:		
Existing business (5% of PP)		$5,000
Start-up business (20% of PP)		$20,000
Required investment for existing business		$30,000
Required investment for start-up business		$45,000

If the business you are buying has a price of $100,000, you will need $30,000 of your own money (equity). If you are starting a new business that is worth $100,000, you will need $45,000 of your own money.

Example #3

	Debt	Equity
Purchase Price (PP) $500,000	$375,000	$125,000
Working Capital:		
Existing business (5% of PP)		$25,000
Start-up business (20% of PP)		$100,000
Required Investment for existing business		$150,000
Required Investment for start-up business		$225,000

In example #3 you will need $150,000 of your own money to buy a business selling for $500,000. If you are starting a new business that is worth $500,000, you should be prepared to invest $225,000 of your own money.

The different working capital levels between starting a new business and buying an existing business is based on the belief that the earning curves are different. How different is a function of your ability to perform and the type of business you have.

Some successful owners believe the business should produce a profit in sixty days, while others say it takes one to three years. In either event when going into business, you should have contingency plans for the unexpected and reserve capital to provide business options.

These examples should help you determine how much money it will take to go into business. Avoid the mistake of starting with a dollar figure based on your liquid assets and then looking for a business you "can afford." Start with your goal, develop a plan, and match your financial resources with the plan.

Business owners generally do not list starting capital as a major hurdle for going into business. Owners and bankers, however, will tell you that borrowing money for an existing business is easier than obtaining money for a "start-up." The frustration usually doesn't set in until you realize that with a little additional capital you could dramatically enhance the position of your business. For example, a large advertising expenditure during the Christmas holidays might increase your sales by a factor of two. This may not have been obvious when you were starting the business. For this reason, the importance of maintaining financial reserves cannot be overemphasized.

Much has been said and written about developing a business plan. More than half of the successful business owners I talked with had not written a structured business plan before going into business. However, they did develop various plans to meet difficult situations. When I informed one businesswoman that developing a cash flow projection was really a business plan, she said, "well I guess I did have a plan: I just thought it was an annual budget." Everyone seemed to agree that a good plan, either in writing or not, was quite fundamental to success.

Several bankers I met with said a written business plan was mandatory for a start-up business if the owner wanted to borrow money from the bank. The requirement often is waived for buying an existing business if financial statements from the business are available and accurate.

There are many obvious reasons for writing a good business plan. The reason most frequently cited is to get money from a bank. I think this is a good reason but not necessarily the best. Being able to articulate your strategy is evidence you understand what is involved.

Bankers need to be convinced that you know what you are doing. A bank vice president told me that he could not have more than 3 percent bad loans in his loan portfolio without attracting the attention of bank regulators. There's a conflict in the whole lending scenario between the bank's limitations (3 percent) and the Chamber of Commerce statistic that 85 percent of small businesses fail. Can you appreciate the bank's quandary? On one hand they feel obligated to support the business community; on the other hand they cannot afford to lose money. Bankers want you to convince them that you will succeed because you know what you are doing and are not among the 85 percent of failures.

If your business is building homes, the chances are the banker knows little or nothing about building nor does he want to. Above all, bankers want to be assured that *you* know. I have watched bankers read business plans. Normally they will ask you to return at a later date, giving them a chance to review the material. But it was interesting to watch those who chose to read the material in the presence of a client. Their interest was captured on the pages bearing the tables, graphs, and numbers. Bankers are looking for facts and other indications that you have quantified your goal. They are not interested in a lot of descriptive rhetoric. A well-developed plan containing accurate facts and figures will go a long way toward gaining the confidence of your banker.

The four main ingredients of a business plan are:

1. Business Description

2. Marketing Plan

3. Financial Plan

4. Organizational Plan

In describing your business, exercise care not to over-describe it. Do not spend much time describing future acquisition goals and expansion plans. Focus on precisely what your business will do in the next year. Avoid technical jargon and present the concepts in clear, concise language.

Example: "I intend to open a submarine sandwich shop on July 1, 1995, at the corner of Lincoln Avenue and Main St. This will be a nonfranchise shop, specializing in soups, sandwiches, and salads. The targeted customer base is people who work in the nearby Industrial Park and normal foot traffic on Main Street."

Developing the marketing plan is extremely important and shouldn't be hastily written. From the moment the banker learns of your business, he or she second-guesses the value and soundness of your idea. Bankers are not necessarily good business people, but they may know the history of subshops on Main Street. A good marketing plan can dispel misconceptions and demonstrate your astuteness in business matters.

Begin with a market analysis, which in the case of the subshop would include the eating habits of your potential customers, their option of other places to eat, and the weak points of the competition. Describe the size of the total market. Do you have to capture 50 percent of the total market to break even? What percentage of the market total are you after?

Next, develop a marketing strategy that describes how you intend to bring customers into your shop. Include your advertising plans and overall techniques of competing with the competition.

The financial plan is what the banker has been waiting for—finally a comfort zone where the banker is at ease. This could be the basis for deciding whether to loan you money. What the bank is really looking for is your ability to service a debt, should they decide to lend you the money, and what collateral you can offer as security.

My first experience with a business loan was a total failure. I walked in completely unsuspecting and attempted to convince a rather bored banker that I was a hard working fellow who loved his wife and children, went to church on Sundays, and therefore was somehow qualified for a loan. In between yawns and glances at his watch, he asked a few piercing questions that I stumbled through with magnificent ignorance. Undaunted in my conviction that I was a good risk and recognizing the only problem was the banker's inability to judge good character, I retreated to my study to plan another attack.

I decided it was best for me to select another bank for my second attempt. This time I approached the secretary, who worked for the loan officers, and asked for copies of all the forms used by the loan officer in reviewing loan applications. Now I was armed with their forms. Included was a balance sheet, an earning statement, and cash flow projections, with the bank's own name stamped all over them. After a few agonizing hours with my old accounting book, I was able to fill out the forms and compose a brief business plan. I will spare you the details, but the second bank granted me a loan to cover the purchase price plus a $20,000 line of credit for working capital.

The difference in the second approach was my willingness to understand the banker's position and comply with his requirements. I had learned to play the game by the rules.

The financial section of a business plan should include the following:

1. Personal Balance Sheet

2. Personal Income Record (past three years)

3. Business Balance Sheet

4. Business Income Record (past three years for an existing business)

5. Cash Flow Projection for the business if it is a start-up (monthly for the first year and then quarterly for the second and third year)

You also should be able to correlate earning activities with marketing strategy. If your cash flow projection indicates an unusual fluctuation in revenue, you should be able to refer to your business plan for an explanation. Also, cash flow should help identify cyclical patterns and trend lines.

When developing the revenue numbers, there is a tendency to be optimistic. Business owners will tell you to be realistic on the "pessimistic side." Don't overstate your earnings or underestimate your expenses. Again, it is better to err on the conservative side when developing the cash flow projection.

You can pick up a monthly cash flow projection form from most office supply stores. You need to become familiar and proficient at asset management and cash projection. As you look at the form, you will notice two columns for each month. The first is the "expected" and the second is the "actual." Each set of numbers will provide the information necessary to manage your assets. Comparing the "actual" to the "expected" will help you identify potential problems and assist in developing your estimating skills. Expenses that are either higher or lower than expected need your attention.

My son, Mark, who is a co-owner and vice president of finance for the Phelan Corporation, tracks fifty-three separate expense items on a monthly basis. He will ask for an explanation from the other corporate officers for any deviation from the "expected," either positive or negative. These tools help manage assets and are critical to success. Mark has not yet sought any bank financing, but in casual conversations with two different bank officers, they both would welcome the opportunity to work with him. Mark has developed a reputation for financial control that will help his corporation obtain financial assistance should they need it.

Before bankers commit their funds, they will most certainly seek assurances that you have thought through your business carefully. A well-thought-out business plan with a detailed cash projection strategy is essential for success. Most business questions need precise answers. Consider issues such as: How much should I spend on advertising? How much should I pay myself? When can I buy a new delivery vehicle? When you are successfully managing your assets, you will know precisely how to answer these questions. In fact, you will be able to anticipate expenditures and minimize "surprises."

Review for a minute what we have covered. In Chapter Two we explored what business might be right for you. The areas of production, retail, and service suggested a method for helping us focus on where the opportunities might lie. In applying your own values and uniqueness, there is a way to capitalize on your strengths and ability to "do it your way" for wealth and satisfaction. In Chapter Three, we looked at the various platforms we may want to consider, i.e., starting a business, buying an existing business, or buying a franchise.

Now let us examine the question, "where shall I begin to look for a business?" In either starting or buying a business, one of the most important considerations is location. Business owners also agree that owning the building or property where the business is located rates high on their priority list. That enables them to transfer a debt payment to an equity gain.

Quite often, statistical data is available from government agencies on traffic count, pedestrian concentrations, and sales tax revenues to assist you in pinpointing the location best suited for your type of business. The City Planning department may have information on future growth projections that would include highways, parks, schools, and business zoning. Take advantage of this information and incorporate it into your marketing strategy.

Finding a business to buy requires patience and persistence. Real estate and business brokers constantly are looking for buyers and sellers. If you know precisely what you want and feel comfortable in determining market value, you may want to consider going through a business broker. There now are buyer brokers who will act as an agent for the buyer, which can be a definite advantage.

Broker fees are normally higher for selling a business than a house. A real estate broker may charge 7 percent for selling a house, where a business broker may charge 10 to 12 percent for selling a business.

The old adage of the "seller pays the selling commission" is more true in the housing industry where appraisal techniques are more refined. When buying a house, the lender will order an appraisal of the property, and depending on the age and location, will accept one of several methods—comparable prices, replacement cost minus depreciation, or construction cost for a new home. The buyer normally is locked into whatever price the lender accepts; therefore the seller must subtract the commission fee for the real estate broker from that amount. The seller pays the commission.

Appraising the value of a business is more difficult because of the "intangible assets," such as the goodwill, patent rights, customer list, or trademarks and copyrights. Since it is highly unlikely that you would find two businesses alike, the use of "comps" (comparables) is not very useful.

It is therefore much easier for the seller to raise the price by the amount necessary to cover the broker commission. So, ultimately the buyer pays the commission when a business is involved, unless he can establish a "fair-market price" and not pay more.

Trained and licensed people will appraise the value of a business, and in some cases the bank will insist upon it.

The cost can be ten times higher to appraise a business than a house, and this cost falls upon the buyer.

An excellent book on the subject of appraising is *Valuing Small Businesses and Professional Practices*, by Shannon Pratt. Published by Business One Irwin.

If you want to avoid the broker commission when buying a business, you may want to consider other alternatives. Newspapers and trade journals are sources of business listings. My preference would be trade journals if your search is not limited to one specific geographic area.

When buying my first business, I talked directly to the owner and used no outside agents. If you use this approach, do not simply walk in and ask if they want to sell. Get acquainted, practice your small talk, find out what you can about the business in general, and then leave. Inquire around town, talk with suppliers and customers, and then visit again. Start by expressing your interest in owning a similar type business and suggest they let you know if anyone is interested in selling. Drop by a few weeks later and see if there is any interest.

Timing is important. If it is a seasonal business, you do not want to approach an owner when the money is rolling in. Stop by during the off-season, tax time, or when you sense the owner may be considering retiring or moving out of town.

Often a business owner may say he is not interested in selling, but they may know of someone who is interested.

Owners have their own network of organizations, friends, golfing acquaintances, and supporters who have their "ear to the ground."

I have counseled a number of people who were interested in buying the business they worked for; this is the best of all worlds. One particular woman was buying an alteration shop from her owner/boss. She was not only the head seamstress, but she kept the books for the owner as well. The owner was willing to help with the financing and remain as an employee. On the surface everything appeared serene, and we were all optimistic about the prospect of instant success. In the follow-up session, problems began to surface. The new owner, who was somewhat passive in nature, had tried unsuccessfully to implement some changes. It turned out the former owner was still running the shop, and the new owner was reluctant to discharge her. After two years, the only business change was the ownership, and that was just on paper. The previous owner was still running the show.

Buying a business or a franchise can be complex, and you should retain the services of a competent legal adviser. In many states, a real estate broker cannot write or exercise a sales contract between a seller and a buyer of a business. A real estate broker can do this for land or a house, but not a business. Check the laws in your state. The seller and the buyer can get together and write a sales contract without anyone else. But only an attorney can act as a third party when business assets are involved.

Business attorneys can sort through various issues, offer advice on transferring ownership, and suggest how you might best structure your business.

You will be inundated with many matters during this period of transition, and it will be comforting to know you have a competent person in your corner reviewing such things as:

- Outstanding warranties and guarantees

- Transferability of licenses and permits

- Extension of lease agreements

- Non-compete agreements

- Valuing inventory

- Accounts receivable

- Accounts payable

- Transfer of business name

- Past-owner consulting terms

- Credibility of financial statements

The attorney also can help determine the best legal entity for your needs, which include, (1) Sole proprietorship, (2) Partnership, or (3) Corporation (C,S,LL).

There are numerous advantages and variations to each of these structure-options. A more detailed explanation, listing the pros and cons, is available at your local library or nearest SCORE office.

An attorney can help determine which is best for you. I cringe anytime I have to pay attorney fees, but it is a small price compared to the cost of a crucial mistake.

5

How to Value a Business

The very soul of the small-business community is the economic value of each business to both the community-at-large and the owners themselves. From entrepreneurs to owners ready for retirement, there is nothing more significant than the fair-market value of the business. Aside from the opportunist, the wheeler-dealer and the high-risk venture capitalist, the process for the entrepreneur to get either in or out of business relies on the "market value."

Like any other transaction in a free-market environment, the buyer tries to get the lowest possible price and the seller is after the highest.

Even when a fair value can be established, the seller may be reluctant to sell, if he perceives the price as not being commensurate with the time and effort given to the business. This is quite typical of people facing retirement age who falsely equate the financial demands of retirement with the selling price of the business. That they built the business from scratch, worked long, hard hours and sacrificed much of their free time, justifies in their own mind a higher price than the market will bear.

The small-business owner may compare the working hours and sacrifices made to run a small business with the eight to five o'clock schedule of the next door neighbor, who after thirty years was able to retire in relative comfort. Most successful business owners will contribute to a retirement program over the years and accumulate a modest savings. Yet their ability to sell the business at a fair-market price is what they are really counting on for retirement. If they were remiss in developing sufficient retirement funds, apart from increasing the value of the business, then they are faced with two alternatives—continue working or sell the business for more than the fair-market value.

On the other hand, people entering the small business community normally are looking for the "best" deal or something affordable and inclined to offer a price well within the boundaries of their own means and often below the asking price.

To the neutral observer, the fair-market value generally is defined as the most probable amount that a business, if offered for sale for a reasonable period of time in a competitive market, would bring to the owner, who is willing but not compelled to sell, from a buyer who is willing to buy.

The definition is an acceptable text book standard; but unlike the sale of land, houses, or commercial buildings the fair value of a business is more difficult to calculate and can be somewhat subjective.

When a potential buyer spots a business that satisfies his career goal and the requirements set forth in the business plan, the inclination is to offer a lower price than asked, "hoping to get a good deal," and leaving some bargaining room on the high end. In the absence of any precise appraising technique, both the buyer and seller will begin the negotiations from a somewhat subjective position.

The real value of any business is based on future earnings. Current and fixed assets as well as past earnings are certainly important. However, the ability of any business to generate future earnings is what ultimately determines its value.

I had the opportunity to talk with a gentleman who had spent most of his working years owning various bars and nightclubs. When we first met, he was in the process of buying a neighborhood bar that by all appearances had seen its better days. What he really was buying, he explained, was a liquor license and the location. Apparently, liquor licenses are difficult to obtain in many locations. He developed a plan for the conversion of this bar into a neighborhood family lounge. He certainly wasn't interested in the dilapidated furnishings and the meager earnings of the present owner.

He ended up paying more than what I would have considered a fair-market value from an owner who was surprisingly reluctant to sell at any price. The buyer certainly wasn't purchasing asset value or past earnings. He was buying his vision of future earnings based on his experience and expertise. In time, the business surpassed his most optimistic projection of future earnings and proved his vision to be correct.

This is an example of applying your own values in determining the worth of a business. Owners sometimes are reluctant to sell a business based on past earnings when they know the profit curve is moving in a positive direction. Having spent years building clientele and reinvesting earnings in inventory, they are inclined to base their selling price on what they perceive the future outlook of the business to be, which again, is a subjective position.

Valuing a business certainly can be based on intuition and seat-of-the-pants economics. More commonly, people will agree to use conventional techniques that are factual in nature.

A starting point for discussing the value of any business generally will begin with the balance sheet. The balance sheet is nothing more than a list of what you "own" and what you "owe," and the difference between the two is what you are worth. If you owe more than you own—you are in debt. If you own more than you owe—you have net worth.

Balance sheets will change from day to day, depending on the activity of the business. So looking at a balance sheet that is six months old is useful only in providing a historical data point, not in determining present values.

Business owners normally update their balance sheets annually for tax purposes, unless they are interested in assessing progress from one period to another. They also may develop a balance sheet for a loan application or in the event the business is to be sold. Reading a balance sheet should be a comfortable experience that allows you an insight into the health of a business. Often the sight of numbers, particularly from a computer read-out, can be somewhat mystical and intimidating. Let's examine the components of a balance sheet and see if we can gain some comfort and confidence in our ability to understand the numbers.

Assets are the first entry and are simply the resources (what we own) of the business. These resources are subdivided into two categories: tangible and intangible. The tangible assets are material things, such as machines, fixtures, buildings, trucks, and computers. Tangible assets will often be divided into current assets, fixed assets, and deferred charges. Intangible assets are those you can't see, such as goodwill, customer lists, patents, and copyrights. Accountants will use variations, depending on the need of the business, but the general format will look something like this:

Assets

Tangible

Current Assets

Cash

Accounts Receivable

Inventory

Total Current Assets

Fixed Assets

Building

Land

Equipment

Fixtures

Total Current Assets

Deferred Charges

Prepaid Insurance

Office Supplies

Total Deferred Charges

Intangible

Goodwill

Customer List

Patents

Trademarks

Copyrights

Total Intangibles

Intangible assets are not commonly carried on a balance sheet unless the business is for sale. As you might imagine, intangible assets are more difficult to value.

Let us continue the discussion of the balance sheet as though we were a potential buyer, interested in gaining some understanding of how much the business might be worth. Incidentally, most sellers will not provide this information unless they are convinced you are a sincere, qualified buyer, or they list their business with an agent who then does the buyer screening.

Starting with current assets in our example, the amount of cash has little relevance as you won't be getting any of it when you buy the business. The only real significance is that it may offer a clue to the level of operating money required to run the business. Cash levels are typically in a state of flux, however, so one data point may not be too meaningful.

Accounts receivable is uncollected money from past transactions that belong to the seller. If the seller suggests they be included in the sale of the business, then there are some things you need to find out. You need to know if any of the receivables have been pledged as collateral? In other words, has the seller borrowed any money and offered the receivables as security? Secondly, you should consider an aging schedule. If any of the receivables go beyond the terms of the sales transaction, they would have questionable value. For example, if the terms were net 30 days and the account has been inactive for 60 days, you may be looking at a bad debt. In this event, you certainly would be justified in offering a lower price to cover the possible loss. For example, if the seller carries the receivable at a full value of $100, and it is thirty or more days delinquent, you might offer $20 for the account and then hope you can collect on it. The best approach, however, is not to include accounts receivable in the purchase price.

Inventory is the area that successful business owners have learned to manage carefully. This will be carried on the balance sheet at cost, which is the amount the owner paid for the goods. Valuing inventory can be a tedious task, but well worth the effort. Aging inventory is another area where discounted value may come into play. Relying on levels of accumulated dust, the owner's memory, or better yet, the purchase invoice, you may discover some inventory has been around for six months or more. There is a good chance it may not sell—so why pay top dollar for it?

Unlike a retail business, inventory in a production environment can mean having products in various stages:

1. Raw material

2. Work in process

3. Finished product

Each step of the process includes varying degrees of labor, based on a standard unit cost, with some level of variance. Variances, normally, will be expensed and/or included in the standard.

Appraising the value of inventory in a manufacturing environment may require hiring an independent expert, paid for either by the buyer or seller.

Fixed assets are material items used in the operation of the business. A consideration when looking at the assets on the balance sheet is understanding how depreciation is being handled. For example, a floral shop purchased a new delivery vehicle three years ago for $15,000. Over the past three years, the owner claimed depreciation of $10,000 and now shows it on the balance sheet at a book value of $5,000. In shopping around for a similar van, you discover that it would cost $8,000 to replace the van with a like model. You then would adjust the book value to reflect the replacement cost—an accurate value from your perspective.

When you as a buyer, look at the value assigned to the fixed assets, you should focus on replacement cost or market value. Appraising fixed assets is less complex than inventory, and your accountant can help you understand the issues associated with depreciation. If you decide to sell your business someday, you will find the Internal Revenue Service treats the difference between the depreciated value and selling price as capital gains, and will tax that amount as ordinary income.

Deferred charges are simply future expenses for which the seller already has paid and wants reimbursement.

Intangible assets, while subjective in appearance, need to be quantified in an objective manner. More friction and misunderstanding arise from discussions surrounding the valuation of intangibles than anything else. The true value of intangibles is their ability to produce future earnings. When we speak of earnings, you should always think of the income statement. Even though intangible assets appear on the balance sheet, their value will be calculated from the income statement.

To illustrate some of the problems in valuing intangibles, we can ask the question—what is the value of a customer list? If it can be used to generate revenue, it has value; if it is used as a Christmas card mailing list, it has very little value.

Calculating the market value of intangible assets will be deferred until we look at the income statement. For now, just be aware that intangible assets will appear on the balance sheet when a business is for sale, and their stated value has no real meaning unless we can appreciate their earning power.

The balancing portion of "the balance sheet" includes liability and net worth, which we need to cover briefly.

Liability follows assets in format and is nothing more than "what is owed." Liabilities are ordinarily categorized as current and fixed.

Liabilities

Current Liabilities

> Notes Payable

> Accounts Payable

> Total Current Liabilities

Fixed Liabilities

> Mortgage Payable

> Total Fixed Liabilities

Net Worth

Total Liabilities and Net Worth

> Total Assets = Total Liabilities + Net Worth

Current liabilities are considered short-term in nature (months), while fixed liabilities are thought of in terms of years. As a business owner, when you add all your liabilities and subtract them from the assets, whatever is left over is your net worth. If there is nothing left, or your liabilities exceed your assets, then consider yourself in debt and working for someone else. To put it mildly, you are in a precarious position.

Another document worthy of your attention is the income statement, which the seller again provides. When starting a business from scratch, the cash projection sheet becomes the income statement, since there is no historical data. In an established business, the income statement is developed from past performance and includes income and expenses for a specific period of time. In order to factor out any cyclical periods, income statements covering a period of twelve months are more meaningful. Monthly or quarterly reports have their place and provide valuable information in understanding the peaks and troughs of a business. It is always useful to view two to three consecutive years of income statements to identify trends and any abnormalities.

Income statements can include as much detail as the owner finds useful. For tax reporting, the IRS demands certain items be reported, while an owner may find additional data helpful in managing the business. It is not uncommon to find active business owners tracking much more than what the IRS requires.

The line items of most interest in the income section are the following:

Income Statement

Gross Revenue (Sales, Income)

Cost of Goods Sold (CGS)

Other Expenses

Net Operating Profit or Loss

Gross Revenue is the total amount of money taken in from all sources. "Cost of Goods Sold" consists of the material, labor, and overhead that goes into any product. The distinction to be made is, "product cost vs. support cost." Support cost is accounted for in "Other Expenses," while product cost is found in the "Cost of Goods Sold."

For example: You own a donut shop and get up every morning and dutifully make your donuts. When the baking is complete, you open your doors and serve the donuts to the waiting customers. The labor you put into making the donuts is a component of "Cost of Goods Sold" (CGS). Your labor in waiting on customers would be included in Other Expenses. Why the distinction and how important is it? The importance is in valuing the inventory, and the I.R.S. insists that you make the distinction.

In the example of the donut shop, there is no real need to make any distinction, unless the owner wants to track the cost, because there is no significant donut inventory at the end of the day. At least the owner hopes not.

Some owners will pay their own salaries at a fixed rate and report it under other expenses, while other owners prefer to take what they need out of the operating profit. Conceivably, an owner could split his salary between "Cost of Goods Sold," "Other Expenses," and "Net Operating Profit."

Both the balance sheet and the income statement should be verified by the seller's tax returns. Since balance sheets and income statements are a snapshot of any particular time period, it is advisable to review the most current information available. Note that the latest tax return may not have the most current financial information, and you therefore would want the seller to provide whatever current data was available.

Banks most certainly will ask for the last three years of tax returns when considering a loan application. With a start-up business, and often for an established business, banks also will ask for three years of personal tax returns in addition to the business returns.

When entering the world of small business, bankers should be viewed as an essential player, along with an attorney and accountant. If the relationship ever becomes uncomfortable, it may be time to change players. A good working relationship will serve you well and is essential for continued success. A common criticism of bankers, mentioned by business owners, was the lack of continuity and tenure of bank staffs. About the time you develop a good rapport with a banker, he or she may have moved to a different branch or into a different position.

Banks view your success in business as an opportunity for them to expand their capital base through payroll, savings and checking accounts, and the opportunity to lend you money in the future. When you do well, they do well, so it's a win-win situation.

The other partner business owners mentioned quite frequently is the accountant. Most owners place the accountant over the banker and the attorney as being crucial to their success. I entrusted our accounting needs to a fellow small business owner who stays current on the changing tax laws and charges far less than many of the larger accounting firms. He works out of his home and is conveniently a phone call away.

If you have any doubt or concern regarding financial matters, rather than "winging it," call your accountant. An accountant can be extremely helpful in matters dealing with the acquisition or disposition of assets, managing profit levels, preparing taxes, and reviewing financial statements.

Emphasizing the importance of a competent accountant is in no way understating the role of the business owner. It is imperative that you become familiar with financial tools and learn to use them in managing your business.

While reviewing the balance sheet of a business with a SCORE client, I sensed his reservation and timidness in getting involved with the array of columns of numbers. Definitely out of his element, he was hoping the moment would pass quickly without any embarrassment. He was giving the appropriate nods and the subsequent "uh-huh," but all he wanted me to answer was whether the business was a good deal. Discipline yourself to go after financial statements as you would any other problem. When someone is explaining a concept to you, whether it be frying an egg or reading a ledger, if it is not clear, ask for clarification again and again until you understand.

In the example of this client, I suggested we compare the balance sheet with a trip to the flea market. Starting with the inventory, and moving through the fixtures, we examined each item by asking two questions: Do you want this, and how much would you pay for it? His enthusiasm began to grow when he came across a 1986 Ford Taurus among the fixed assets. His eyes lit up and he shouted, "what the hell do I need with a car?" He began to write a list of questions for the seller and some action items for himself. Among the furnishings were some desks that he felt were important, but the price needed to be verified.

In the end he was pouring over the document making notations, and I was the one nodding *my* head, saying, "uh-huh."

We then turned our attention to the income statement, which had been prepared by the seller's accountant. His first suggestion was, "let's have my accountant look at this and see what he thinks." I responded by saying, "that's a great idea, but let's take a minute and see if there are any questions we might have." Just out of curiosity, I asked, how much of a salary is the owner drawing? He grabbed the document and said, "Hey that's damn important; Where would I look for that?" Within minutes, he was jotting down questions and rummaging through papers like a tax accountant on April 14th.

We concluded the review by comparing the seller's tax returns with the income statement prepared by his accountant. The projected income for the current year appeared to be 50 percent higher than the reported earnings for the previous year. If things were that good, why was the owner selling? The business broker handling the sale had told him that the owner wanted to pursue other business interests. In light of the income statement, something seemed wrong; more questions needed answers.

Our session lasted an hour and clearly demonstrated two points: Reading financial statements is not that difficult and knowledge is power. Two weeks had passed and the client had called for another appointment. I could detect enthusiasm and a new level of confidence as he suggested we discuss an offer he wanted to make for the business.

The client had inventoried his personal attributes and financial resources and decided he wanted to invest no more than $60,000 of his money as equity, retaining an additional $25,000 as reserve capital.

Our discussion began by first considering the purchase of this business as an alternative investment opportunity. In the heat of battle, it can be difficult to separate emotions from facts; he was clearly excited and committed to having his own business. But was this business a good financial investment?

The business certainly would pay him a living wage in exchange for his work. But that should be viewed as a separate issue. He could work for someone else and have that benefit. The investment under scrutiny was the $60,000. If you are going to spend money just to buy yourself a job, you are either very wealthy or very foolish. Because in addition to a wage, you are also entitled to some return on your investment (ROI) over and above any wage you may draw.

If you were to put the $60,000 into a bank account, certificate of deposit, or money market account at today's rate, you would draw somewhere between 3 and 5 percent annually, and would probably sleep well at night, knowing the principal and interest were safe.

The same $60,000 invested in a balanced mutual fund could average 8 percent to 12 percent annually over a period of years. With the dynamics of the equity markets, you might lose some sleep.

Purchasing rental property with the $60,000 offers another alternative worth considering. With income and appreciation, an annual return of 6 percent to 8 percent is certainly possible.

In each of these alternatives the return should be consistent with the risk. Buying a lottery ticket is the ultimate risk; the chance of ever seeing your money again is infinitesimally small but the possible return is enormously high.

In noting earlier advice to avoid unnecessary risks, the business investor will want to take measures to secure his investment principal.

The projected rate of return for any business investment is somewhat subjective. However, the range commonly required when investing in a business is 15 percent to 20 percent annual return on equity. Investing $60,000 in a business should then produce a profit (over and above the owner's salary) of $9,000 to $12,000 annually.

Remember that if protection of the principal is one of our investment objectives, then we must settle for less return. We know that investing our $60,000 in a federally insured bank account will produce an annual return of $3,000, representing a small return with no risk. Small business owners are inclined to be more conservative than you might imagine. While a 50 percent annual return has a lot of appeal, it also comes with a risk factor few business people will accept.

If I were to invest $60,000 in a business that had few tangible assets of any salvageable value, I would want a high rate of return (50 percent). Because in the event the business were to go under in two or three years, I would want to take steps to recoup my $60,000. An example of this type of business investment might involve copyrights, patents, customer lists, or in some cases vending routes where the machines were either leased or so unique there would be no general market for them.

On the other end of the risk range might be a well-established hardware store with a very salable inventory in a community of economic growth. If the business also included the two-story building on Main Street where the store was located, my $60,000 would be more secure. Because of the salvage value of the assets, I would be willing to settle for a lower rate of return (ROI), perhaps in the 10 to 15 percent range.

Somewhere in the financial section of your business plan, you need to address your anticipated ROI and why you feel it's appropriate. If you are thinking about buying a specific business or starting one from scratch, look at the adjusted profit, before taxes, to determine if the business is capable of meeting your goals.

If the answer is "the business should start showing a profit in a few years," know that your investment of $60,000 has been placed under the mattress. A dormant investment or one based on some future development is not always a wise investment.

If however, your plan is to return earnings back into inventory or buy more equipment and not show much profit, then that's a conscious decision to utilize your profits in a productive way. When we use the word "adjusted profit," it includes earnings going back to increase equity; or earnings taken out as profit. In either case, it's a positive return on your investment.

When considering a business investment, some distinction needs to be made between business and nonbusiness assets.

Let's examine the example of buying the hardware store. If the two-story brick building on Main Street was a part of the deal, then you are really buying two things; a viable business and a commercial building, all packaged into one transaction. For financial planning, there is a need to separate the investments and determine the value of each based on its own merits. If the hardware store occupies 2,500 square feet of space, determine what the going occupancy rate is on Main Street. Charge the hardware store that amount and credit the same amount to the building.

When buying into situations like this, there is a quandary facing most buyers: Is the income from the business sufficient to service the package debt? A good example is purchasing a farm near the edge of town. The value of the land may have escalated with urban growth, and presently the best use of the land is homes, schools, and factories. It's not realistic to sell the property to a young farmer and expect the profits from farming to be sufficient enough to buy the premium property.

Sellers also face this problem when disposing of their businesses. Long-established greenhouse and nursery businesses, which have experienced city growth around them, discover that their land is worth more than the business. Owners find themselves paying property taxes based on residential and not agricultural rates, and realize that liquidation probably will be to a land developer and not another greenhouse grower.

Identifying the investment is clearly the first step you should take, whether it be a start-up or an existing business. You must be able to distinguish between business assets and nonbusiness assets. Even the farmer must decide if the crop revenue is sufficient to buy the land. In some cases, you may find a business where the profit can service the purchase of the building and the land. This would be an excellent way to use earnings to increase your net worth and build up a retirement fund.

Let us now examine a method for determining the fair-market value of a business. It is quite simple and we will only need two numbers for the calculation.

The first number is the easiest to acquire. What rate of return (ROI) do you want from your investment? Given the risk factor, what return do you need to protect your principal?

As we have discovered, the range is quite broad, and the selection can be somewhat subjective. Having considered such things as risk tolerance, asset salvage value, projected future earnings, and alternative investment opportunities, suppose you pick a ballpark range of 10 percent to 15 percent. That means you expect a 10 to 15 percent annual return on your equity investment. Anything less than 10 percent is not acceptable.

The second point needed in the calculation is the annual adjusted profit before tax. Creative bookkeeping used by so many business owners makes this number difficult to determine. They have an aversion to paying income tax just as you and I, so the trick is to keep the reported profits as low as possible. There are two ways of doing this—keep the revenue low or the expenses high. On the revenue side, deferred billing may help, bartering is done, and some owners will pocket the money and not report it. Failure to report revenue is illegal, unethical, and just bad business, but it does happen, particularly in businesses dealing in cash transactions.

On the expense side, owners will spend money (which otherwise would go into reported profits) to buy equipment, pay bonuses, expand inventories, and generally update the business. This is all perfectly legal and doesn't bother the IRS in any way. This increases the owner's equity, and sooner or later the government will get its cut. The owner hopes later rather than sooner.

A good accountant will help you "normalize" the reported profit figure by ensuring the revenue and expenses truly represent the activity of the business. If the owner is working and not drawing a salary, the profit needs to be reduced by some number to accurately reflect the cost of the owner's contribution. Start-up businesses often will use the spouse's outside income to support the family expenses and not draw any income from the struggling young business. This is a common situation, but in analyzing the financial health of the business, some accounting is necessary to compensate for the owner's labor contribution. For example, if the owner was working 40 hours a week and not drawing a salary, that would represent an unreported cost, and consequently the reported profit would be artificially high.

The owner may also be listing payment on the land and building where the business is located as expenses. If the building has unique features, such as grain storage or a commercial greenhouse, you may have no choice but accept the payments as a valid business expense. On the other hand, if you are buying a hardware store and part of the expense is payment on the building, which exceeds what you might normally pay for rent, you may have some reporting options.

The objective is to account for all of the revenue and all of the expenses necessary to run the business. The difference between the two is the profit or loss that you can expect to realize.

By using the following relationship, you can determine the value of a business based on its profit and your ROI expectations.

$$\text{Fair Market Value} = \frac{\text{Annual Net Operating Profit}}{\text{Return on Investment}}$$

For example: Given an annual net operating profit of $15,000 and an ROI target of 15 percent, you should not invest more than $100,000 of your money in the business.

$$\$100,000 = \frac{\$15,000}{15\%}$$

If you invest more than $100,000, you will be making less than 15 percent on your investment.

When presenting financial statements for loan approval, the bank will take notice of the operating profit as the source that will service their loan. The bank may or may not go through the exercise of normalizing revenues and expenses. The responsibility is yours to point out any extenuating circumstances that impact the net operating profit.

When borrowing money, it is advisable to adopt a monthly installment payment program. Even if the bank offers period terms, it would still be advisable to offset monthly revenue with monthly expenses. You also need to adjust the net operating profit by adding the scheduled loan payments back into the expenses of the business.

For example: The bank agrees to loan you $50,000 for 15 years at 8 percent interest and wants monthly installments. Your payment would be $478 a month or $5,736 a year.

If the annual operating profit had been $15,000 prior to the loan, it now would be reduced to $9,264 ($15,000-

$5,736). Assuming you still were willing to invest your $100,000, we see now that the return on your investment has dropped from 15 percent to 9.3 percent.

$$\text{Return on Investment} = \frac{\text{Net Operating Profit}}{\text{Fair Market Value}}$$

$$9.3\% = \frac{\$9,264}{\$100,000}$$

In the example above; if the $50,000 you borrowed went into the purchase of the building, and assuming you can service the debt from earnings, you have added substantially to your worth by buying both the business and the building, so the 9.3 percent annual return might be totally acceptable.

Taking the net profit from the income statement and dividing that number by your ROI requirements gives you the amount of money you should be willing to pay for that specific business. Now you know precisely what the worth of the business is, based on its ability to generate profit. The only challenge in the exercise is to ensure all revenue and expenses have been properly accounted. Now we are ready to compare this number to the balance sheet entry entitled "Total Assets."

"Total Assets," which include all of the tangible and intangible assets, is the dollar amount the seller feels the business is worth. If the total asset number is smaller than the investment value from our calculation, it indicates the earnings are sufficient and the price is favorable. If the total assets are larger, you need to know why. Do the assets include nonbusiness assets, such as a building? Are the intangibles unreasonably high in terms of earnings?

With the information we have, we can now place a value on the intangible assets by subtracting the tangible assets from the fair-market value, calculated from the income statement. Whatever is left represents the earning value of the intangible asset. Remember the intangibles (good will, customer lists, copyrights and patents) have a real value based on future earnings. If the operating profit from the income statement does not reflect enough earnings to support both the tangible and the intangible claim, then you start wondering. Are the tangible assets valued too high, or are the intangible claims unrealistic? Going back to our flea market mentality: Why would we pay for anything that doesn't give us earning potential?

Remember *the real value of any business is its ability to generate future earnings*. Why would you pay for any assets that don't produce future cash flow?

Another way to put a dollar value on intangibles, such as location, business name, established clientele, customer lists and patents, is to consider adverse consequences. If you didn't have any of these things, how much business would you lose and for how long? Intangibles do have some intrinsic value, either positive or negative.

When you see a sign in a store window claiming new ownership, the name and reputation of the former owner apparently had a negative value.

The adjusted profit number from the income statement could show a loss. Unless there is some logical explanation, such as a one-time write-off, a natural disaster, or some revenue altering event, you are buying a business to lose money.

When discussing the market value of a business, one caution is not to let the seller slip his arm around you and with a wink and smile tell you the numbers are really better than they look. Better to walk away from deals like that. Competent accountants can examine the financial records and offer an independent point of view that may keep you from making a costly mistake. It's the seller's responsibility to present the financial history of the business that accurately reflects all of the financial activities.

6

How to Arrange Financing

When counseling people who are interested in owning their own business, particularly those with little prior experience, the first question that generally comes up is, "where can I get some money?" Experience in buying a home has conditioned us to think banks will lend between 80 to 90 percent of the market value and allow 20 to 30 years to repay the loan. There also is a misconception about the Small Business Administration (SBA) being a willing and able agent that will lend money to anyone in the small business community. Also, newspaper articles often quote sources willing to identify government programs and policies aimed at supporting the small business community. Obtaining money is not difficult, provided you have a worthwhile program, but it is not quite as simple as some would have you believe.

The more fundamental question is, "what can you afford to borrow?" To listen to an enthusiastic entrepreneur describe plans to open or buy a business that is valued at $150,000 with only $5,000 of his own money, is disheartening.

In Chapter Four we discussed a method for determining how much of your own money you should invest and how much in borrowed funds it would leverage. This is very important! Along with determining how much to invest initially, we also established guidelines for reserve capital.

Have you ever visited a gambling casino and watched people play the roulette table? I am always intrigued by the number of chips people are willing to commit on any one spin. They must have some underlying strategy such as, "if I won big on even numbers last time, I will shift to odd numbers this time and reduce my bet." Then you see a conservative player (probably an accountant) who bets one chip each time on either red or black, and after two hours is $15 ahead.

A stockbroker recently tried to convince me to "diversify" into a mutual fund plan. He suggested investing in a growth fund, an international fund, and a bond fund. He offered this as a means of covering all bases. The logic was that if one goes down, another will go up. Why not buy just those on the way up? Isn't it the broker's job to help me pick winners and avoid losers? Why play the game of "averages" with the hope of breaking even?

Investing in a business should not be a gamble, and a good plan will help you not only avoid loss but also allow you to do better than average.

Our previous model on investment limits (see Chapter Four) suggested leveraging your own money by finding a lender willing to lend you money on a 3 to 1 ratio. That is not to suggest that taking on debt is advisable, but merely a possible option open to you.

If you can borrow money at 8 percent, invest it in your business, and realize a 10 percent return, then it's probably a good business decision. If you borrow money at 8 percent for a nonproductive activity, it might be considered a bad decision.

Starting your business with just your own money may be virtuous and something worth doing, but it isn't always a good economic decision. Unlike investing in a house, your business will generate money, and the revenue should be proportionate to the investment.

Use the format of the cash flow projection and analyze the available options before making a final decision. The precise amount of money you can afford to borrow and the exact terms you can handle will jump right off the page. You certainly don't want to walk up to a banker and tell him you need about $5,000 for as long as you can have it.

Let's assume your analysis suggests that additional funds would make a difference. You have determined exactly the amount you need and are confident the revenues will justify the investment.

The question then becomes, should you introduce the additional funds as a debt load or equity investment? And does it make any difference?

When the owner(s) invests money, it is considered ownership, worth, or equity. There is no obligation to pay it back, and it entitles the owner(s) to the right of decision-making and a share of the profits.

In a sole proprietorship, one person owns and runs the entire business. In a partnership, there can be more than one owner and more than one person running the business. The partnership arrangement also can provide for more than one owner with only one person running the business (silent partners). Corporate arrangements are much the same as partnerships, allowing multiple owners with an appointed few actually running the business. Equity equals owner-ship, and the owners decide who runs the business.

In raising money for a business, whether it be debt or equity, a major consideration is the element of control. If you were to receive money from a family member, would there be any strings attached? The benevolent father, who lends $5,000, then imposes his judgment on the running of the business, can be a real detriment (to put it mildly). He is trying to have it both ways.

A venture capitalist normally will insist on an equity position before lending money. He is exchanging capital for ownership and a voice in running the business. Banks, at one time, played an active role in the running of the business as a condition for lending money. This has changed.

Asking lenders for advice and opinion is still a good practice, but having them involved in the day-to-day operations as a condition for granting the loan, is, fortunately, a thing of the past.

Bankers became involved initially to protect their investment. If a firm borrowed money for plant expansion and instead invested it poorly in the stock market, the bank might end up out in the cold. So getting involved in managing the business was a way of protecting bank capital.

Today's bankers are no less interested in securing their loans, but now they seek collateral as a means of security rather than trying to run the business.

You should give a great deal of thought to the debt versus equity question and understand thoroughly the effect it will have on your business, particularly in who manages the business.

One exasperated business owner was relating how the banks had tied his hands. He couldn't do anything because the banks had secured a second mortgage on his home, were holding his receivables as collateral, and were about to repossess his delivery truck. He blamed the bank for all his grief, but I suspected that he was the source of his problems. Banks like well-managed, successful businesses and are wary of those with management or financial problems.

Owners with an equity interest tend to be more motivated in achieving success than a creditor with a secured position. Everything comes back to control and how you want to run the business. I came across an interesting arrangement with a sixty-year-old father and his thirty-five-year-old daughter. She was the technical expert and wanted to run the business. His contribution was investing his capital and keeping the books. They lived in separate towns and were quite compatible as long as the distance was maintained. They formed a partnership with the agreement that when he was sixty-five, he would sell his half of the partnership to the daughter, with terms extending over a ten-year period.

As the independent third party, I thought she was getting the better deal. There was no provision for securing his investment other than trust. Should the business fail, who had the most to lose? This is the litmus test most lenders look for when determining whether you have enough ownership interest to warrant their getting involved.

In Chapter Four we discussed the importance of maintaining reserve capital and developing lines of credit before going into business. Once again, consider your options and distinguish between debt and equity before making any final decision.

In preparing for this section, I talked with various people in the lending community: six different loan officers from commercial banks, two loan officers from a federal credit union, one venture capitalist, two loan officers from a farm co-op, one investment banker, two private investors, and one loan officer with the SBA.

Once you get past the rules and regulations of the lenders, you find an interesting diversity, not only between institutions, but also within the same institution. One commercial loan officer placed a lot of credence in a well-written business plan. A fellow officer in the same bank viewed it as "nice to have," but not mandatory. I hasten to add that nine out of the eleven loan officers interviewed said they would insist on a business plan for a start-up business, while four out of the eleven said they would require a plan for an existing business. All eleven agreed that new business owners should develop some formalized plan, if only for their own use.

Most of us view the banker as "the keeper of the money." They are the ones we must confront and hopefully convince that we are capable of running a business successfully and thereby qualify for a loan. We perceive the lenders as being in a position to either make or break our dreams. So with hat in hand and some degree of reverence, we approach this bastion of capitalism in the hope it will smile with favor on our financial needs.

In talking with both bankers and business owners, however, you will discover these perceptions simply are unfounded. Here are some general observations shared by bankers and business owners you may find helpful in developing your own strategy.

1. Many new arrivals on the scene are unaware of how the lending process works. They "fight the system" rather than work with it.

2. Bankers are human and subject to personal biases and doubts like anyone else.

3. Successful and potentially successful business owners never feel they are "asking" for money, but rather presenting a win-win situation for the business and the bank.

4. Before presenting a loan application to a bank, most bankers would welcome the opportunity to sit down and discuss your ideas and offer suggestions as to how you might proceed.

Let's examine some of these observations in more detail. Banks and businesses share much in common. Each bank has its own comfort zone, area of expertise, and internal quirks. People run banks, so each bank has its own distinct personality. Banks have to show a profit to satisfy their owners and will avoid getting into bad or questionable deals. Banks want to please their customers and are eager to work with them to improve the economic health of the community.

Banks have only one product—money. They strive to offer convenience and friendly service to entice customers to use their product. When a bank lends you money, it may insist you maintain your business accounts with them. This, of course, enhances the banks profitability, which keeps it competitive and enables it to offer more services at better rates.

As a business person, you should become familiar with the bank's products, or the various types of loans they offer. Not all loans are the same. Here are some examples:

Short-term loans, often called a revolving line of credit, allows you to borrow the amount you need, when needed, up to a certain amount. It's similar to a credit card. Banks usually ask you to secure these loans with collateral, such as fixed assets or accounts receivable. If you are in a seasonal or cyclical business, you may find a need for a short-term infusion of cash, and this would meet the need. You should not set the limit any higher than what you are going to use. The more money the bank reserves for your use, the higher the cost to you. Most lines of credit are expected to be paid back within a year.

Intermediate term loan is used most frequently for a business start-up, the purchase of a business, buying equipment, or expansion capital. Again, the bank will ask for collateral to secure the loan and will seek monthly or quarterly payments. The loan may be extended for a period of three years.

Long-term loans can extend for periods of ten to fifteen years and are used for the same reasons as the intermediate loan. Banks are inclined to add more provisions and look for more collateral when granting a loan for a longer period of time.

Commercial mortgages might be needed if you plan to build or buy land and buildings. Banks generally will lend 75 percent of the appraised value of the property, which can be amortized for a period of up to twenty years. Banks probably will insist on an independent appraisal, which probably will be at your expense. If you already own property, you may mortgage your property as a means of offering collateral. If the property already has a first mortgage, then you need to remember that the rates on a second mortgage generally are set higher than those on the first mortgage.

Letters of credit would be the bank's promise to grant a loan or guarantee a payment under certain conditions. Suppose you purchase a piece of property on the outskirts of town, for example, and then decide to have the property annexed to the city. As a condition of the annexation, the city might ask for evidence that you will pay for sidewalks and curbs when they are later constructed. You can pay for the improvements at the time of annexation or provide a letter of credit from the bank stating their willingness to guarantee the funds when the city is ready to begin the work. Such a service from the bank may cost you $50 to $100, but would avoid the need for spending several thousand dollars as a prepayment for the work.

Consulting with a banker will help you determine the type of loan best suited for your needs. In purchasing a business involving real estate, two or more loans might be required; a commercial loan extending over a period of twenty years could be used to purchase the building where the business is located. A second intermediate-term loan might be granted to purchase the business equipment and inventory. Conceivably, a third loan providing a revolving line of credit for operating capital would complete the package. After your bank has reviewed your needs, it will be in a position to discuss all of these options.

Processing loan applications is handled differently by various institutions. Larger banks may use their branch offices as filters to screen out the obvious rejections, forwarding the remainder to a centralized loan committee to determine the merit of the loan. The loan officer with whom you deal may only have the authority to say no; approval of your loan will come from people you may never meet. This may seem cold and impersonal, but the final approval is made on the strength of your loan application—regardless of who reviews it.

In a smaller bank, your loan officer also has the authority to say no. Here again the final approval must come from the loan committee. The difference at the smaller bank is that the loan officer probably will be a member of the loan committee, or at least will be able to present your application personally.

In either case, the front-line officers know precisely the criteria for acceptance and will not submit a loan application that has no chance of approval. When recalling the five "C's" of banking, the application of "character" (good or bad) might be more of a determining factor in a smaller banking environment.

The committee reviews are not automatic—it is not like punching numbers into a digital lock with only one right combination opening the door. The committees are made up of people with opinions, feelings, fears, and biases. If, for example, they had approved five loans in the past month for dry cleaning businesses, they may not be inclined to approve another—independent of its merit, at least for awhile. Perhaps they had a recent closure on a restaurant, and they may not be anxious to take on another one. Unfortunately, there is no way you would know this in advance. Your loan officer may have some inclination and yet elect to submit your loan, hoping for approval. You may never learn the real reason for the rejection and walk away thinking poorly of your financial strategy.

Here are some general tips from bankers on how to improve your chances for approval by the loan committee:

1. Select a bank, either small or large, that is actively seeking small-business customers. You will find that some banks are making small-business loans while others are avoiding them.

2. Spend some preliminary time with the loan officer reviewing the loan information, and acquire some feeling for the bank's position on your type of business.

3. Shop before selecting a bank. Find out how active they are in support of community affairs. Compare their financial position with others in the community.

4. If you are turned down, ask what you could have done differently and would they consider a resubmission.

I discussed these problems with a loan officer who also served on the loan committee. He revealed that his bank was quite active in lending money to small businesses, and in a candid way he mentioned a few things his bank looks for.

His bank prefers lending money to established businesses with a history of earnings and solid assets. If you are going into business, you will find it easier to borrow money to purchase an existing (profitable) business than for a start-up. On the purchase of an existing business, his bank would consider a debt to equity ratio as high as 80/20.

His bank preferred lending money to small manufacturing firms, which sell both inside and outside of the local economy. Again, the loan officers look for a solid inventory and fixed assets. They seem to avoid businesses in the retail, service, and restaurant sectors.

When lending money to start-up businesses, his bank looks for a minimum investment by the owner of 30 percent and a debt to equity ratio of 70/30. A well-thought-out business plan is a must, and they suggest leaving a copy of the plan for the banker to review. Do not expect to have your plan read while you are present. The officers found most owners to be optimistic to a fault—the bankers' private joke is to use half of the projected earnings and twice the projected expenses if you want something near the truth.

The loan officer said that in recent years, more weight was being given to the applicant's character, particularly in the smaller banks. A good credit rating reveals much of the character and will be examined closely.

"Special Assets," a term commonly used by bankers when referring to bad loans, always is in the back of a banker's mind. They will take every precaution to ensure the safety of their loans. Their insistence on collateral, owner equity, and expertise gives testimony to the concern they have for both your success and theirs.

Business owners with whom I spoke felt it was important to establish a good relationship with a banker. Some felt more comfortable with older bankers, some sought out women, and some mentioned getting the bankers out from behind their desks, such as a lunch meeting. Most conceded they were matched with a person the bank felt was appropriate.

From the loan officer's view, I asked for those qualities in a borrower that gave them a sense of security and a willingness to consider a loan. Their views certainly differed, but there was some common ground they shared. For example: First impressions are important. The well-dressed person seems to convey both respect for the moment and a professional attitude. The person who can articulate in clear, concise terms and focus on the important issues is one who most likely will get the banker's attention. Avoid the temptation to shove piles of material under the banker's nose. Voluminous material can stifle the flow of conversation and is more useful left as "support documentation." Some bankers may ask for specific information, and your ability to produce it quickly, without rummaging through heaps of paper, is impressive. Let the banker establish the agenda and set the tone. If he misses something you feel important, do not hesitate to mention it. If his enthusiasm does not match yours, don't be offended; this may be a first for you, but he has heard similar stories from countless others. His interest will be no less diminished if your proposal is sound.

Once you have provided the necessary information, loan officers will require time to sift through the details and digest all the material. A loan officer may have three or four applications on the desk at any one time. Be patient, your loan will receive due consideration.

Bankers often will arrange your financial information in a standard format for a comparison. If your business is a hardware store, they will want to know how you compare with other hardware stores. In making this comparison, they rely on data found in an annual publication entitled "Annual Statement Studies," which is published by Robert Morris Associates (RMA), Philadelphia, Pa. This book contains a compilation of performance numbers for every type of business in the United States.

The data in this book has been arranged by size of revenue, both past and current. At a glance, the banker can compare your projected earnings and expenses against hardware stores with similar revenues.

When making the comparison, bankers will focus on the assets and liabilities that we covered in Chapter Five. They also are interested in comparing performance ratios. Depending on the type of business and whether there is historical data versus a start-up business, bankers may use one or more of the following ratios to determine the financial soundness of your particular business.

$$\frac{\text{Total Current Assets}}{\text{Total Current Liabilities}}$$

$$\frac{\text{Cash and Equivalents + Trade Receivables}}{\text{Total Current Liabilities}}$$

The following ratio is a measure of the number of times the inventory is turned over during the year and can help in understanding merchandising problems.

$$\frac{\text{Cost of Sales}}{\text{Inventory}}$$

This ratio reflects the amount of owners equity invested in fixed assets.

$$\frac{\text{Net Fixed Assets}}{\text{Tangible Net Worth}}$$

The following ratio expresses the relationship between debt and equity.

$$\frac{\text{Total Liabilities}}{\text{Tangible Net Worth}}$$

There are numerous other ratios bankers may find useful when assessing the strength of your business. In making the comparisons, bankers aren't scoring you on a pass-fail basis, but rather trying to understand your strengths and weaknesses.

Successful business owners have learned the value of the RMA publication, not only for developing loan applications, but also to better manage their own businesses. Successful owners say it is not enough to know the answers—you must anticipate the banker's questions. Reviewing this publication with your banker will better prepare you for the realities of the banking world and help you focus on the more critical items.

Your loan officer may require additional information or clarification before reaching a decision. If your loan meets the preliminary requirements, the officer will then submit it to the loan committee for approval. If the loan application does not meet the preliminary requirements, you will be advised. Repeated phone calls inquiring as to the status of the loan will serve no purpose. Allow two weeks, and then contact your loan officer if he hasn't called.

The question of loan guarantees from the Small Business Administration (SBA) may come up in discussions with your banker. It is generally up to the bank to determine whether the loan should be submitted to the SBA for guarantee approval. The borrower may request the bank consider that option, but the bank probably will take a position independent of the request. Remember, the SBA does not lend money, it simply guarantees loans. There are some exceptions, however, and you should discuss the exceptions with your banker, a SCORE counselor, or the SBA.

The general rule is if a bank turns you down, most other institutions will too. Several business acquaintances expressed their preference for credit unions, while another found a helping hand from a farm co-op. Some borrowers swear by small banks while others prefer the larger, full-service banks. Whatever your choice, the procedures are fundamentally the same.

Once you have established credibility with a particular lending institution, stay with it. Moving your accounts around can send a message of instability to the lending community. If a problem arises, discuss it with your banking partner and search for the solution together. If moving the account is the best answer, let your bank know what you are doing and why. I have more than once regretted burning a bridge that could have served me later.

Another source of funds is family or friends. Many business owners get their start this way. The reviews are really mixed on this subject. As one owner said, "If it's not bank-worthy, why subject Aunt Mildred to the risk?" Other owners have an affinity for paying the interest to family members rather than the banks. There was agreement on keeping everything at an arm's length when bringing "family" money into the business. Draft a promissory note, specifying all the terms. Set the terms equivalent to the bank rates, and guard against default. The other contribution family and friends often make is to offer labor. When family members work, pay them whenever possible. Such businesslike arrangements can prevent family trouble later.

Recalling the concept of "control" when debt or equity is involved could not be more crucial than when family members are involved. Debt at the hands of family or friends may end up appearing more like ownership (equity) because of all the unsolicited advice and opinions. Weigh the alternatives carefully before accepting family money.

The use of another person's money is a common practice in a capitalistic system. Most successful business owners know how to leverage their equity and manage their cash flow. A reputation for good management and an impeccable credit rating will open doors of opportunity both in financial circles and with reputable suppliers.

When dealing with bankers, the key to success is understanding the banking process and developing a partner relationship. Become familiar with the banker's position and needs. As a business owner once correctly stated, "I don't ask for money, I share an opportunity."

7

Running Your Own Business

In concluding the interview with various business owners, the last question was, "would you ever go back and work for someone else again?" The answer always was a resounding "never." For perhaps the first time in your working life, you will find owning your own business offers an almost eerie sense of freedom. In retrospect, owners felt their personal growth had been stymied while working for others and did not really blossom until they owned their own business.

One successful owner said, "when working for someone else, I felt like two different people." She felt compelled to dress and behave appropriately for her employer, yet when she was away from work, she was able to be herself. Owning her own business resolved this internal conflict, and now she enjoys a sense of oneness and personal growth.

Your business will reflect your own personal standards and values. Others will see "you" in every aspect of the business. Your sense of quality, fairness, treatment of employees, work ethics, and concern for customer satisfaction will all be "your signature."

Once you gain control of running your business and establish a routine, you will find both comfort zones and sources of stress. Contrary to preconceived ideas of what it is like to run a business, you may find there are some areas that demand more attention than you had imagined possible. Some owners report that half of their time is spent in inventory management, while others find personnel matters occupy most of their time. The time-consuming sectors most mentioned by business owners include:

- Record keeping

- Inventory

- Marketing

- Employing others

- Financial strategies

Here are some thoughts on dealing with these issues from owners who believe they have mastered them.

Record Keeping

Owning and running your own business will be a continual learning process. There will be trial and error, good days and bad days, and moments when you feel very much alone. Begin early to collect information on business performance issues by recording problems, solutions, and results.

It will not be obvious in the beginning, but the day will come when a good historic data base will be worth its weight in gold. Part of the learning process will be measuring the consequences of past decisions. For example, if you advertise in the local newspaper, you would record the size and cost of the ad, the circulation of the paper, the product advertised, the weather on the day the ad ran, and what response you had. Nothing elaborate—just a simple diary entry. Inevitably, the question of using the newspaper will come up again, and reflecting on past experiences will help you make the right decision.

This record keeping should be informal and not time consuming. It was amusing to hear so many owners say record keeping was vital to success, and then admit to their own shortcomings in keeping records. Relying on memory was a bad idea, they added.

There are other records required by taxing and licensing agents that need to be more structured and maintained on a regular basis. They, too, are really quite simple. You are probably aware of the I.R.S. position on maintaining records for income tax. The same applies for a business. Not only must you substantiate each claim, but you must retain these records until the statute of limitation for that return runs out. For more information refer to the IRS

publication 583, entitled "Taxpayers Starting a Business."
Each of your revenue and expense entries on the tax return
must be supported by some recorded documentation,
whether it be a computer disc or a written journal. Employment taxes, such as, Social Security (F.I.C.A.), Federal and
state withholding tax, Workman's Compensation, and
unemployment insurance should be recorded as not only
proof of payment, but to assist you in projecting future
costs. If your business is engaged in selling a product, then
you will be collecting a sales tax, which once again should
be documented. This may all sound very demanding and
somewhat complicated, but once you establish a routine it's
quite simple. In the twenty-plus years I've been in business,
I could count on one hand the number of times any taxing
agent disputed or questioned my numbers. And it sure was
comforting to have solid records to fall back on. More
importantly, I regularly refer to these records for projecting
the future of the business.

Buying an established business can offer the advantage
of an existing bookkeeping system with the possible training from the previous owner. However, let me share an
experience I had in this regard. I purchased a business with
a bookkeeping system in place, and the previous owner
provided several hours of instruction in how to maintain the
records. After three months of posting faithfully in a very
routine fashion, I was able to summon enough courage to
take my books to a certified public accountant (CPA). My
question to the accountant seemed simple enough—"am I
doing this right?" Well, he got on his soapbox and for the

next thirty minutes I took notes on balancing accounts, reconciling journals, tracking ledgers, and preparing taxes. I came within a breath of saying, "I'm confused, would you please do this for me, Mr. Accountant?" Which is exactly what he wanted me to say. The only reason I didn't say it was that I feared his next question might be, "Do what?" My ignorance then would certainly become obvious. Instead, I returned to my business and continued for another two months to "post my books." Finally, another accountant came to my rescue. His calming manner and insistence on keeping it simple helped me to distinguish between numbers and concepts. His questions were always the same, "what do you want to know about the business?" and "what's important to you?" He would then add, "here is what the government needs to know, and this is how you should record taxes for payroll and sales." In less than one hour we had revamped the entire bookkeeping system. Now I had something that was functional, meaningful, and above all, simple. The centerpiece was a double entry journal with supporting ledgers for revenue, payroll, accounts receivable, and accounts payable. I would post my invoices and sales transactions to the ledgers daily, and then transfer the information from the various ledgers and checkbook into the journal once a week. The journal is nothing more than a diary for recording the financial history of income and expenses. With my new bookkeeping system, I was able to answer questions from customers, suppliers and bankers without first digging through piles of paper. I was organized and in control, and had time for other important matters.

Taking over someone else's books may be beneficial in some cases, but not always. Starting a business from scratch forces you (or someone else) to develop a system to match your specific business needs, a process that has some merit.

Many businesses are not large enough, in my estimation, to require anything more than a simple manual system. I consider the task of bookkeeping an exercise in staying familiar with not only financial transactions but also with customers and suppliers. It should take about fifteen minutes each day to update the ledgers and about thirty minutes a week posting to the journal.

I've noticed that my son Mark is spending considerably less time with the business record keeping than I did. And in addition to what I was doing, he also puts out a monthly statement, tracks twice the number of transactions, and handles check writing with a computer. At the end of the year he hands the tax accountant a computer disk instead of my revered ledgers and journal. This process has become a standard business practice.

If you have computer capability, by all means look into software, such as *Quick Books* and *Quick Pay* and countless others. Since the introduction of fax machines and computers, the distance between bankers, accountants, and business owners is only a keyboard away.

Whatever system you use, get the bookkeeping organized to fit your needs before opening the doors for business.

Learn to meticulously record every expense and revenue on a regular basis.

Several owners attributed their financial success to a conservative accounting system. For example, when you collect a sales tax on your retail transactions, the temptation is to combine all sales revenue, including tax, into a single account. A better approach is to separate the tax portion into another account, ensuring the prompt payment of the taxes. It is not necessary to open different bank accounts for all of these accruals; it all can be handled with a simple bookkeeping entry. The money itself may be in a single checking account, but remember the balance in the checkbook does not necessarily reflect "available" funds. It is similar to your personal checking account. If you have a balance of $750 in your account, and a house payment of $600 due in two weeks, common sense would tell you not to go out and spend $700 on a piece of furniture, thereby jeopardizing the house payment.

I am aware of two automotive repair businesses forced to close their doors because of shoddy bookkeeping practices. One business obtained permission from the IRS to delay tax payments, which eventually became too large to handle. The second business spent every dime it took in, making no provision to pay taxes, insurance, payroll, or rent.

Just remind yourself, as the money starts to roll in, that the checkbook balance is not an accurate gauge of your liquidity. If the temptation becomes too great, open a business savings account and move some funds out of your sight, or discipline yourself in good bookkeeping habits.

Inventory

Inventory management can make the difference of three to five percentage points in your net profit. While not always crucial for the service industry, it is extremely important that manufacturing, wholesale, and retail businesses control the costs associated with inventory.

Conceptually, it seems simple—don't stock what you don't need. Business owners, however, are optimistic by nature and often will view excess inventory as a security buffer, a hedge against inflation, or an equity position. These same owners often will declare, "what I need is a good marketing plan."

Manufacturing firms generally do the best job of controlling inventory levels. Their ability to project usage and scrap levels enables them to control· production by establishing intermediate and long-term needs. Manufacturing companies and their suppliers often will form partnership agreements for their mutual benefit. It is less expensive to carry raw material than the finished product because of the labor content and inventory tax associated with the finished product. For this reason, the raw material supplier may be more willing to carry inventory than the manufacturer of the finished product, and they may even agree on sharing the carrying cost. The raw material supplier is only one link in the process. They in turn look upstream to their suppliers for inventory agreements. Everything would run smoothly if only the final consumer would be more predictable, and here is where the problem lies. If the Ford Motor Company knew, with any degree of certainty, that its customers would buy exactly one million blue Thunderbirds next year, it could produce precisely that number and at less cost. Managing inventory is a juggling act for most, and understanding the customer is the best approach to managing inventory correctly.

At the opposite end of the spectrum from the manufacturing firms are retail businesses. The owner of a sub shop shared his problems of forecasting bread needs from one day to the next. Even with refrigeration, day-old bread does not sell. He had developed historical data that would suggest his bread need for Saturdays was sixty-five loaves. Each week he found he needed sixty-five loaves to get his shop through Saturdays. One Saturday a school bus full of high school kids, en route to a football game, entered his shop and began ordering sandwiches. He was in deep mayonnaise! The next week, having recovered from the bus incident, he was back to his predicted sixty-five loaves per Saturday. But on a Saturday several weeks later at 11:30 a.m., the skies opened and a torrential downpour lasted until 2:30 p.m., keeping people from his shop during the critical lunch hour. Now he was up to his buns in bread. Is there no justice?

Jerry Mollica seconded this frustration and said that his deli has learned to network with other restaurants to get through these types of crises; "We share everything from cheese to pans to survive."

How do you anticipate the customers' needs and develop a good inventory model? Historical data and marketing forecasts are the best tools available. Historical data will come from your record keeping (diary), and forecasting will be your best judgment of future events. But neither is infallible.

The owner of the small gift shop with more than 2,500 different items relied on her intuition. She had two factors in her favor: ten years of experience and a willingness to think as a customer. Her shop had heavy tourist sales and strong Christmas holiday sales. Spring and summer were lighter, yet the demand was every bit as pronounced as the two major seasons. In total, she was dealing with four distinct opportunities—each being a little different from the other. Her challenge was turning the inventory every ninety days. Certain basic items had year-round appeal, and she had learned to display slow-moving items near the cash register for the impulse buyer. Also, she advertised for the annual end-of-year sale each January. To control this fast moving inventory she devised a simple manual system using 3x5 recipe cards. Each item coming into the shop was recorded on a card with a beginning inventory quantity and a date. Before placing the card in the metal container she would cut off the upper right-hand corner of the card. At the end of each day she would sit down with the little inventory box and carbon copies of the sales tickets to reconcile the inventory. For example: If a painted clay pot had sold, she would locate the index card for that item, reduce the quantity by one, and then date it. When the quantity on-hand reached a certain predetermined ordering point, she would turn the card upside-down when replacing it in the file box. At a glance she could tell from the position of the cards which items had to be reordered. A very simple, yet effective technique for tracking inventory.

She thought her inventory problems had more to do with quantity than selection. In time she had learned what was "trendy" and what her customers preferred. Suppliers, however, offer quantity discounts to entice retailers to buy more. Although three items may be sufficient, purchasing six offers a 10 percent discount. The question is to buy the three you need, or go for six and discount the retail price? Experience will help you make these decisions, and a good record system will expedite your learning process.

Remember that inventory is equity, similar to a savings account, and so it's your investment dollars sitting on those shelves. If the inventory is good, however, it represents future earnings. One merchant said, "if you don't have it, people can't buy it." However, if your money is tied up in slow-moving inventory, it will limit your options of bringing in the "hot" items that are now selling. You are thus drawing very little interest on your equity. Inventory issues generally consume much of the business owner's time because it is often the company's largest asset.

Marketing

Selling your product, whether it be service or retail items, is the heart of success for the small-business owner. Similar to inventory management, marketing should be driven by customer satisfaction. The best way for a small business to expand profits is by increasing its customer base. So, if you are to be successful, it is extremely important to understand the needs of your customers. It is easy to be egocentric when it comes to determining customer needs, a phenomenon not unique to small businesses. Recall the early 1970s when Detroit persisted in producing gas-guzzling cars. Purchasing a new car every four years was the "American way," or so Detroit believed. The customers didn't think so, and the foreign competition was quick to recognize and seize an opportunity.

One recurring message successful business owners emphasize is, "think like a customer," who would begin by asking, "what would I like and how much am I willing to spend?" Examine your merchandise or whatever it is you sell in relation to their prices and ask yourself, "is this a good deal or not?" Shop the competition and see what is available! If you are honestly convinced of the value of your product, you may rest assured customers will seek you out. Value sells itself, and word of mouth is a powerful advertising tool and should never be underestimated.

I frequently visit a small out-of-the-way café, located in an old two-story converted house in a quiet residential area. The owner is a woman who worked with me for years in corporate America before striking out on her own. I have never seen any advertisement for the café, and yet she manages a full house daily. People will seek out the unique and unusual and relish in sharing their secret with others. At a recent social gathering, my wife and I, who seldom eat out, sat dumbfounded as others revealed the names of eater-ies, bakeries, and other secluded "finds" that they would gleefully proclaim as the "only place to go." The owners of these establishments had selected a passive approach to marketing and had chosen instead to rely on the strength and reputation of their product.

Word-of-mouth advertising infiltrates more slowly and may not reach all of the potential customers; nevertheless it is effective and inexpensive. Customer loyalty can be difficult to understand and quite disappointing at times. The small merchant who stands by helplessly as customers move their business to the large chain stores should not despair. Competing with large department stores and twenty-four-hour grocery stores will be an exercise in futility if you elect to play "their game." As part of your market analysis (see business plan), two questions should have been answered: "What does the competition offer?" and "What don't they offer?" If they offer selection and low prices—don't compete in that arena. Place your emphasis on quality, service, location, friendliness, and other things not offered by the competition.

Market your strengths by letting people know what your edge is over the competition, and repeat your story as often as possible. Identify funds in the cash projection exercise for a continuing advertising program, and carefully monitor the results.

A real estate agent was reviewing a survey form from one of his clients. In the section aimed at finding out how the client located this particular agent, the client had checked off "radio." The agent had not advertised on the radio for more than nine months but had just spent a large sum of money on television commercials. He was rather surprised and concluded that buying a home certainly wasn't an impulse item, and in such cases the response curve to an advertisement may extend beyond nine months.

Advertising is only one aspect of product marketing. How you display your product—whether it be manufacturing, retail, or service—will impact customer acceptance.

A small software firm found success by taking the following steps: Before visiting a potential customer, the owner first would seek out as much information about the client's business as possible. Secondly, he would develop ways of making that specific business easier to manage and control through his company's software application. Finally, he would look for ways to increase the owner's profitability, which would make the software programs more appealing and affordable. Finally, he would approach the potential customer with a personalized product. Thinking as a customer, and not as a software salesman, allowed him to customize a proposal, complete with the owner's name and some relevant applications for the customer's consideration. He demonstrated to the customer a caring concern, which distinguished his business from other software firms.

Have you ever visited garden-supply stores that feature running water, fountains and fish ponds, quaint little bridges, and blooming flowers everywhere? By suggestion, they have tempted customers to duplicate that environment in their own back yards.

Soft music can be heard in the waiting rooms of doctors' and dentists' offices, intended to soothe the nerves of the apprehensive patient.

Antique stores create a "used" setting, from the old-fashioned bell on the front door to the manual cash register—all intended to develop the feeling of nostalgia. These are all props used to put the customer at ease and stimulate the buying instinct in all of us.

Those in manufacturing must go out to their customers. Small firms generally will rely on a network of established distributors or agents who handle multiple accounts. Motivating these people by providing financial incentives is the key to success. A product that sells itself and is in big demand is always the salesperson's delight. One that requires some selling effort may need more financial compensation to motivate the salesperson. Intermediate to larger firms will employ their own field agents, and here again, compensation is the name of the game. Setting a quota and establishing territories will be an ongoing balancing act.

More than ever before, the opportunity for world trade offers the small business owner a chance for expansion and increased wealth. If your products or services have done well in this country, the same basic strategy may be applied to foreign markets.

Currently, only a small percent of American manufacturing firms export overseas, despite our government's willingness to help. The International Trade Administration (ITA), with district offices in sixty-six U.S. cities and 125 overseas posts, can supply specific export information. For example, if you need to know how your products are selling worldwide and which markets are growing the fastest, the ITA has the answers.

The Export-Import Bank of the United States maintains a special office to provide information on export credit insurance, and direct and intermediary loans extended to finance the sale of U.S. goods and services abroad. The toll-free number is (800) 424-5201.

For additional information, contact the United States Department of Commerce, or your local SCORE chapter.

Employing Others

Most small business owners will employ people to help run the business. The owner's goal is to find people willing to share both the pain and gain as the business grows and prospers. Most employees will buy into the gain aspect of your goal and leave the pain for you. Remember that employees are your representatives and are perceived by the customers as being just that. A rude employee will damage your reputation with resulting business losses, while a friendly, competent employee will earn you money.

Since you cannot do everything and be everywhere, the people working for you should be an extension of your values and beliefs. Given that expectation, it will be your responsibility to instill in your employees those precepts and work ethics you feel are important. There are three steps in developing good employees:

1. Selection

2. Training

3. Delegation

4. Teamwork

Selection

Selecting the "right person" is something you will learn with experience. When interviewing, ask yourself, "could I work with this person, or for this person?" Evaluate the human chemistry that is occurring and rely on your instincts. Identify physical limitations, willingness to work overtime and weekends, and salary requirements. Offering minimum wage for the single parent of three children would not be a good basis for a lasting relationship. Understanding their needs and employment goals is essential in the selection process.

Training

Establishing expectations and a comprehensive training program is the greatest service you can offer the employee and yourself. The competent employee is a business asset who will make a lasting contribution to your business and provide a service for your customer. Train employees in the skills required to perform their tasks, even when they say, "I've done this before." Share your philosophy on business and customer relations with them. Remember that training needs to be an ongoing event with periodic follow-up, which includes giving employees an opportunity to offer feedback and express their opinions.

The crowning endorsement will come when you feel comfortable in allowing the employee some space of his own. A good employee is a valuable asset, one who will help your business prosper. Develop and maximize the employee's skills to the point where he or she can assume not only responsibility, but a certain degree of authority. One measure of success in accomplishing this delegation is observing who the employee interacts with before starting his or her workday. If you find the employee seeks your guidance or direction daily, the leash is probably pretty short. Well-trained, self-motivated employees are difficult to find and retain. Show your appreciation for their contribution by meeting their personal growth needs and providing fair compensation.

Benefits

Small firms ordinarily have limited benefits, but the absence of any program may seriously hinder your ability to attract and retain good personnel. Some benefit plans are legally mandated such as, social security, worker's compensation, and unemployment compensation. Other health and welfare programs may become less optional in the future, but presently they are used sparingly in the small-business community. However, smaller capitalized firms have an opportunity to offer their employees a number of meaningful benefits. Employees, like the owners, need to feel appreciated and be able to relate to the business on a personal level. Some benefits found in a small-business environment would include:

- Paid lunch, along with morning and afternoon breaks

- Employee purchase plans

- Paid vacation and holidays

- Time off for funerals and jury duty

- Cash bonus based on profit

- Use of company truck for moving or hauling personal items

- Group medical plans

- Free meals in the restaurant business

Owners also have the opportunity to select from several retirement programs for their own benefit. When going into business for yourself, there is always the fear of ending up without any medical or retirement benefits. The truth is that there are a number of very competitive programs available. Bankers, insurance companies, and stockbrokers are a good source of additional information. Be aware that there is no "halfway" when offering benefit programs to employees. You can't compensate a few selected employees and ignore the rest. If a program is offered to any employee, it must be offered to all employees.

A comprehensive benefit program should not be thought of as a financial burden or a social obligation, but rather as a good business investment to attract and retain good employees. In sharing your success with employees, you once again extend your value system and indelibly write your "signature" for all to see.

Teamwork

In a business where there is close employee interface, it is important to develop a team environment. Hearing employees say, "we're just one big family," is a good indication of a healthy working relationship. When employees work together, there can be a synergistic effect, which means that the combined efforts of all the individuals is greater than the sum of their individual efforts. Building a strong team involving owners and employees is just plain good business sense. When you develop your business philosophy, include a section on how you want to treat customers, suppliers, and employees.

Some owners interviewed favored the idea of hiring either contract labor or temporary employees. This pattern has been growing steadily since the early 1980s and definitely has found a niche in the workplace. In recent years the IRS has taken a stronger stand on the use of contract labor. Unfortunately, its position was made necessary because of employer/employee abuse. The ruling is still evolving, but currently an employer can hire contract labor to perform tasks not requiring his direct supervision for work that falls out of the normal business description. Work such as facility maintenance, janitorial work, and security are examples of contract labor. Temporary or seasonal employees are treated differently by the IRS as they are hired for peak workloads and then dismissed. These people would be under the direct supervision of the firm, unlike the contract labor. In both cases the advantage to the employer is that employees can be added "as needed" and released with no explanation or advance warning. Also the employer often pays no direct compensation benefits. One drawback, owners report, is the lack of personal bonding between the contract and temporary labor and the regular business employees.

Successful owners also have commented on the question, "what would you avoid doing if you were to start your business over?" The answers ranged from, "I would never go into business again," to "I should have done this years ago." The answers were all pretty general in nature. Several said they would stay away from family involvement, while others said they would avoid partnerships. One woman attributed her failed marriage to the business venture. My words of compassion were met with, "the business gave me more satisfaction than he ever did."

Financial Strategy

While many business owners spoke freely of the virtues of borrowed money, there also was strong sentiment in support of financial independence. The need for start-up capital and short-term working capital were acknowledged by most as being a common and reasonable request. The opposition heard most often was against long-term debt. Professionals in the field agree that a business with an indebtedness beyond fifteen years bears the blueprint for disaster. The reasoning for this conclusion is that earnings should be sufficient to finance natural growth, and "controlled budgeting" should be the mechanism for keeping costs contained. Long-term debt (15 plus years) goes beyond the scope of projecting the business earnings with any degree of accuracy, and the question of servicing the debt becomes a concern. The case was made for "growth through earnings or no growth at all." One businesswoman said, "if you're not doing well, why do more of it?" Some owners pointed out the difficulty in making money with borrowed money, given the movement in interest rates. Another owner said he would love to purchase a piece of equipment at a cost of $150,000, "but if I can't justify a return on my investment within seven years, I'm just kidding myself." The message to avoid "long-term debt" was loud and clear, long-term meaning anything greater than fifteen years.

The goal of avoiding taxes by keeping business expenses high through spending can be a double-edged sword. If your business has developed a strategy for expansion or the acquisition of another business, include in that strategy a method for internal financing. Some outside borrowing may be appropriate, however, particularly if it can be matched with internal funds. The method for accruing internal funds is through retained earnings. This means money is set aside each year from the net operating profit. This is not particularly good advice without some plan for reinvesting the money. To save just for the sake of saving, or the "rainy-day" mentality is questionable economics. If your business is capable of generating 15 percent net profit each year, an amount still greater than most safe alternative investment opportunities, then by all means reinvest in the business. If you see the opportunity for expanding your business, meaning a 15 percent profit on a larger base, then expand.

Remaining Flexible

It's good advice today to stay flexible. Not only are most markets dynamic, but customer tastes and your competition are always in a state of flux. I recall watching helplessly as Meg's office supply slowly went out of business. Having patronized this small business over the years, it was disconcerting to see her give up the market share to the larger discount stores. This small family-owned business seemed to work hard in offering good service at reasonable prices. As a customer, I observed the store's inventory levels dropping noticeably in the final months. When items were not in stock, Meg would always offer availability the next day, with delivery at no extra charge. Meg complained of the increasing number of competing office supply stores and her customer's lack of loyalty. Something was changing and it wasn't Meg. Unable to sell the business, she had a final liquidation sale to pay off the creditors and then shut the doors. Meg and her family had practiced the same business methods in the last week of business as they did years ago. The reasons for their failure may have been many, but my suspicion was that the world around them changed, and they didn't.

Staying competitive requires an ongoing market analysis to stay ahead of the competition and to understand the customer needs. Suppliers and vendors often can provide valuable information on what is moving at the wholesale level, which is an indicator of customer demand. Stay abreast of the market by visiting the competition, attending trade shows, surveying customers, and just plain getting away from the business to see what is going on around you. Follow community affairs and network with other business owners.

Running your business successfully will require your efforts in both the internal operations and being able to run with the competition to sustain your customer's loyalty.

8

Keeping the End in Sight

Bill Sawyer had twelve years of service as a truck mechanic for Hank's Auto. His occasional back problem did not prevent him from doing some of the best work in the garage—until the day it became so painful he needed help getting up from the "creeper." In the months that followed, Bill realized that a career change was something he had to consider. No longer able to work at his trade, he would still spend hours "hanging out" at the garage, visiting with Hank and his wife Betty in the office. One day Hank asked, "Bill, why don't you buy this place; I'm ready to retire?" That's how Bill got into business and Hank got out.

The transition worked out well for both Bill and Hank. In fact, Bill is now thinking of retiring in ten years. Bill will tell you that buying a business from your employer is "the only way to go." He already is giving some thought to selling the business the same way.

By thinking ten years ahead, Bill is the exception because most business owners do not seriously consider selling their businesses until the very last moment. They may have given it a passing thought from time to time or have been tempted by the occasional offer from the walk-in buyer or real estate agent. But owning a business is more than just a job, it's a way of life, so getting out of it can be difficult.

There is a number of reasons for an owner to sell a business. Be aware that unsuccessful owners may offer any number of reasons, none of which may be true. The evidence suggests the "real" reason for selling a business falls into two classifications—successful owners and unsuccessful owners. Here are some of the bona fide reasons you may hear:

Successful Business

- Poor health

- Retirement

- Reached a financial goal

Unsuccessful Business

- Losing money

- Fed up with the public

- No personal life

- Buying another business

- Moving to another state

Take comfort in that the financial statements of the business will normally lead you to the proper conclusion, independent of any reason the owner may offer.

If you are the owner of a successful business, you should allow three years to prepare the business for sale. If your business is unsuccessful, you should have gotten out yesterday! A case certainly can be made for the well-managed business always being in a state of readiness and requiring no special effort to prepare it for sale. The only question would be, "Is the owner ready?"

If you are an owner and thinking of selling a business, reverse your role for a moment and think as a buyer. If you were the buyer, would you be getting a good deal? Another question to ask yourself, "Would I sell to a close friend or a relative, and at what price?"

The key to success for getting out of business is quite similar to getting into business. Begin by developing a comprehensive plan that addresses the major issues. You should consider these action items before selling the business: prepare the business, prepare yourself, and then go look for a buyer.

Preparing your business for sale, aside from the aesthetics, can begin with the financial statements. Starting with the balance sheet, you should attempt to place the assets in the best possible condition. Begin by asking yourself these questions:

1. Are the equipment and fixtures in good repair?

2. Does the inventory include any obsolete material?

3. Are the receivables current, and have the bad debts been written off?

4. Are you currently carrying any fixed assets that have no real business value?

5. Can you accurately quantify the intangible assets?

6. Have you discussed with your suppliers the continuity of terms, should a new owner take over?

7. Are your accounts payable current?

8. Will your lender agree to the assumption of any long-term debt?

9. Is your lease agreement assumable?

10. Can you transfer license agreements?

11. Are there any personnel issues that need to be dealt with?

Now review the income statement and ask yourself these questions:

1. Do the records for the past three years accurately reflect all of the business revenue and expenses?

2. Is the business showing a profit?

3. How does your business performance compare with others, using the RMA publication as a standard?

The next considerations when selling a business are your plans for the future, both personal and financial. When Hank and Betty sold their auto shop, they agreed to finance the sale. This gave them a monthly income at a tax rate less than a lump-sum settlement. In addition, they stayed on for several years as consulting employees, which provided them with a small income and meaningful work. Any seller should start arranging his personal finances well in advance. Plans also should be made for establishing personal goals, whether it be retirement or another business. Should the buyer insist on a noncompete agreement, how would that impact your plans?

The last consideration in selling a business is finding a qualified buyer. There are some owners who phase out of business simply by liquidating their assets and closing their doors. Most, however, will attempt to find a qualified buyer to continue the operation of the business. By planning ahead, you may be able to identify your successor from among your own employees, a customer, or even one of your suppliers. Identifying a key employee and then developing his skills in preparation for ownership can provide you with much personal satisfaction, not to mention the advantage to the employee.

Circulating a fact sheet to reputable competitors, suppliers, and even customers has worked for some sellers. Normally, a casual comment to people who have shown an interest in your business is all that's required.

Two owners of a boutique business had worked hard for years to build their business and were approaching retirement when one partner died suddenly and the other became seriously ill. Unprepared, the surviving partner was forced to put the business up for sale during a time of economic recession. Unable to find a buyer and without strong management, the business faltered. The best of plans may not have helped in this situation, but in the final days the owner was left with few alternatives.

As you develop and establish your business, also develop the skills of your employees. A well-managed business will never allow itself to get into a position where its future depends on any one person. Develop managers and possible successors capable of running the business in the absence of the owner. If you are the only one allowed to blow the whistle or run the train, you will find it difficult getting away, even for a brief vacation.

If you own a family business, and there is some interest in passing the ownership on to your children, you may want to consider gifting the assets. This offers distinct tax advantages in estate planning. One convenient method for accomplishing this is to form an S corporation and gift the stock to the children each year. Each parent can make a $10,000 per year, tax-free gift to each child. Discuss your goals with a tax accountant regarding other limits and considerations. Your attorney can advise you on "buy-sell agreements" and other legal issues.

If all attempts at selling the business to family, friends, or associates fail, then you should prepare to go public with the sale. Begin by having your accountant update the financial statements, then talk with your banker regarding available financing, and with your attorney about listing agreements and sales contracts. (Ask your attorney and accountant about their fees beforehand).

Having gathered all of this information, you should now be ready to look for a buyer. Here's where to begin.

The easiest way of testing the waters is by turning to the local newspaper. Newspaper ads are effective in attracting both local and national interest and are quite affordable if you stay with a modest ad. The newspaper published in the capital of a state is read by many outside the state, and so the circulation becomes national. Your local newspaper may have some circulation outside the immediate area, particularly if you live in a popular place. People often will select a locality in which to live, and then search for the business. If you live in the "garden center" of the world, your ad will attract buyers regardless of the type of business you have. If your particular location is lacking in national appeal, then you must rely on the strength of the business opportunity.

Ads placed in trade journals are another option. They are national in scope and read by people interested in your specific type of business. Check with those publications dealing in your specific type of business and see if they have a classified section.

Screening the serious, qualified buyers may be your next task. There always will be people interested in owning your business, but few will have the financial resources to buy it. Your discussions with your accountant, banker, and attorney will help you define the qualifications necessary to meet the terms of purchase. If, for example, you decide on owner-financing and advertise that fact, you will attract legions of prospective buyers. If, on the other hand, you ask for a cash sale of $250,000, you may feel like the Maytag repairman. The way you word the ad, based on your established selling terms, can be very useful in screening out the nonqualified buyers. So word the ad to attract only those people who can qualify to buy the business.

You should prepare a preliminary fact sheet in advance, giving the economic climate of the area, and a business description which includes size, age of business, and any unique potential. Also provide a description of the product and a brief financial statement. There should be nothing on the sheet you wouldn't be willing to share with suppliers or competitors.

Should a serious buyer ask for additional financial information, be prepared to supply a current balance sheet and income statement, along with the last three years of tax returns.

Some prospective buyers may break the inner screen and obtain all the detailed financial information without being qualified to buy the business. It's a tough decision to determine what qualifies a person and how much verifying is justified. In general, sellers tend to be somewhat lax in this area, particularly if they have nothing to hide and are anxious to find a buyer.

If a buyer shows an interest and verbally begins to test your price or terms, stop the dialogue and insist that the person submit an offer in writing. This will accomplish two things: A written offer constitutes an agreement to purchase, and it eliminates any buyer who is not sincere. With a written offer, you can discuss rejection, acceptance, or a counteroffer with your accountant or attorney.

Owners who have sold businesses, advise others to get as much agreement as possible with the buyer on the critical aspects of the sale before hiring an attorney. The best of all worlds is to reach agreement between a buyer and a seller and then pay only one attorney to draft a sales contract. This avoids the "your and my" attorney loop which can be costly and unnecessary.

Another avenue for finding a buyer is through a sales broker. Real estate or business brokers list your business and relieve you of the time-consuming responsibility of advertising, screening prospective buyers, finding financing, and locating attorneys. These agents will ask you to sign an exclusive listing agreement for some specified period of time (six months is common), with the stipulation that you will sell through them at the sales price you agreed

upon. Agents often will have a list of qualified buyers looking for a business to buy. Going through an agency offers
expediency, convenience, and allows you time to run your
business. Some business brokers will offer an appraising
service, at a nominal fee, independent of your signing a listing agreement with them. So there are some definite advantages to listing your business with a selling broker.

The drawbacks of going through a listing agent begin
with cost. Expect to pay anywhere from 10 to 12 percent of
the selling price to the agent. They may try to demonstrate
that this cost is really paid by the buyer—and they may be
right. It will depend on establishing a fair-market value and
then whether the business is sold for that amount.

Agents normally will rely on the owner for support in
two crucial areas: owner-financing and selling support. If
you are willing to "carry back" a note for a portion of the
selling price, it could make the sale more likely. Secondly,
an agent will rely on your business knowledge to convince
the buyer of the merits of the business.

Some business brokers are very knowledgeable in the
area of appraising value and will not list your business
unless it is properly priced; others will take any business at
any price. When talking with a broker from California, he
revealed a table of ratios used in his area, a table that gives
suggested selling prices as a percent of gross revenue. For
example, floral shops should sell for one-half of their
annual gross revenue. Be aware that some appraisals are
more reliable than others. One appraiser told me that a

good rule of thumb is "never to use a rule of thumb in appraising!"

Be cautious if an agent offers to list your business for sale at what you know is an inflated price. The agent may offer assurances of having a list of eager, cash-laden buyers. But your business could be tied up contractually for the duration of the period specified in the listing agreement. If your business does not sell quickly, the agent may then suggest a reduced price or other concessions.

You also may be approached by a buyer-broker. This is an agent acting on behalf of some buyer, unlike the listing-broker, who is acting as an agent for the seller. The buyer-broker may receive a fixed fee directly from the buyer or a percent of the selling price from the seller.

In recent years we have seen the emergence of a "facilitating agent" who represents neither buyer nor seller. Often this agent will ask for payment prior to listing your business, in exchange for pledged efforts to bring qualified buyers to your doorstep. This approach is generally found in the rural areas. Read the fine print and contact references who can confirm performance.

From these various approaches, you should select a selling technique that you are comfortable with and that you feel confident of the results. Unless there are extenuating circumstances, I would start by seeing what I could achieve on my own before enlisting the support of others.

An alternative to selling your business is direct leasing or the hiring of an operational manager. This would be similar to renting a duplex you owned or finding a property manager to handle your rental property. This arrangement is common when there is a large amount of depreciated assets that could result in large capital-gain tax, if the business were sold. If you owned the building where the hardware store was located, you might find that selling the business, with a twenty-year lease on the building as a condition of the sale, might be best for all parties.

Instead of selling the restaurant you own, find a competent manager to run the business, and then live off the annual profits. Like property-management firms, there also are business-management firms that may be willing to run your business for a share of the profit. Much will depend on the size, location, and profit of your business.

Of course, there are risks involved in having someone else manage your business; your personal reputation and the good name of the business are but two examples. Your attorney can be helpful in providing legal safeguards to protect both you and the manager.

Through the SCORE office, I counseled a couple in their early sixties preparing for retirement. Over a period of twenty years they had built a business, founded on a patented invention. They were strongly attached to this unique business and the very thought of selling or abandoning it totally was somewhat repugnant and difficult for them to deal with. Their solution was to franchise! With the support of an attorney and banker, they began to search for a way of developing a franchise network that might keep the business concept alive.

At last report they had sold two franchising rights and were considering three other applications. The owner/ inventor felt he would be making more money in retirement than when he actively worked the business. Granted, his role had become more administrative, but now he was teaching and training others to succeed, which provided personal satisfaction and offered the hope of keeping his invention alive.

There are hundreds of examples of successful franchises that had humble beginnings. H. & R. Block Inc. now has more than 8,800 offices worldwide, of which approximately 4,800 are operated by franchises. This network is so extensive that there are few new territories available. Purchasing an existing office now sells at a premium price. So don't overlook this option, and perhaps, rather than selling your business, you may want to think about expansion through franchising.

The final method of getting out of business is simply to liquidate. A case of how it can be done successfully so everyone benefits is covered in the following experience.

A medium-sized machine shop decided ten years ago not to invest in computer-aided design (CAD) systems. The technological update would have been too costly and promised only marginal returns, in the opinion of the aging owners. They made a conscious decision to continue with what they had, recognizing it was a calculated risk. The gamble didn't pay off, and today they are closing the doors, shutting down the operation of a thirty-five-year-old business. As part of the decision not to upgrade their machinery, the owners also developed a contingency plan to deal with any adverse consequence of that decision. Implementing that plan now has become their salvation and demonstrates the maturity of their management skills. Employees have been counseled on a regular basis regarding the state of the industry. In some cases, class work was subsidized and employees, particularly the younger ones, were encouraged to seek different employment. Buyers were found for many of the larger presses, small machinery was auctioned, and bids were accepted for both raw and scrap material. The property, including two acres and several buildings, was listed with a national real estate agent. By working closely with several loyal customers, they were able to establish an agreement with a competitor that called for hiring six of their key employees in exchange for the owners' written endorsement to their customers in support of the competing firm.

The owners walked away with an adequate retirement fund, the employees were looked after, and their customers' concerns were addressed. The reason for their success through the years, and even in the end, was good planning and concern for both customers and employees.

Owners often will lose sight of the people who made their business success possible, namely, the employees and customers. When going out of business, whether it be selling, franchising, or liquidation, develop a strategy to provide for others. Remember, your "business signature" is a reflection of your values. Now, more than ever, is the time to demonstrate those principles that made you successful.

Summary

Owning your own business offers a unique opportunity for accumulating wealth, for personal growth, and for work satisfaction. By showing an interest in this book, you have already displayed a characteristic behavior found in successful business owners—the willingness to change.

The process of acquiring your own business begins with determining "where you are," and defining "where it is you would like to be." Unfortunately, most people never move beyond the daydreaming stage. However, the serious entrepreneur is willing to make changes and recognizes the adverse consequences of not changing.

Each of us has a unique perspective on life, based on our value system, education, and experience. What you can offer the business world is different from anyone else, and that very difference is what you should capitalize on. In starting a business, the obstacles may seem insurmountable. But it is essential to face the challenge, a decision requiring courage and perseverance.

After talking with successful owners in more than thirty-five types of businesses, it became obvious to me that their combined experiences held the key to success. With so many good examples to follow, there is less need to be apprehensive about facing the unknown. Following the example of owners who have succeeded is one way of enhancing your own chances for success. Not surprisingly, I found the owners interviewed were willing to share all of their experiences, including failures and successes. Why not benefit from their experiences and emulate success?

The following are some types of businesses that were included in the survey:

Accounting and Tax Service

Alterations and Sewing

Arts and Crafts

Auto Repair

Auto Supply

Bar

Business Broker

Coffee Shop

Computer Repair

Computer Software

Desk Top Publishing

Donut Shop

Earth Moving/Excavation

Electrical Supply

Florist

Gift Shop

Golf Shop

Greenhouse /Nursery

Hardware Store

Home Repair

House Painting

Liquor Store

Manufacturing

Music Store

Nightclub

Office Supply

Pet Supply

Printing

Property Management

Restaurant

Television Repair

Textile

Vending Route

From such a diverse group, the comments ranged broadly and represented a variety of opinions. There was, however, a unanimous agreement on several points that the business owners felt fundamental to success. Consider these as you begin your own adventure in the world of business.

Know Your Business. Understand your product and the customer's needs. Without this background, you are certain to fail. Work for someone else first if necessary, but do not start a business without this basic knowledge.

Hard Work. Sixty hours a week is a common requirement for success. Interestingly, the owners seldom referred to this time as "work," but rather as "time spent on the business."

Persistence. Work through problems and master those difficult tasks you would rather avoid. Always work with diligence and patience, and never sidestep any issue.

Business Plan. Whether it be formal or informal, develop goals and a strategy. Marketing, finance, and organization will require detailed planning if you are to succeed.

Organization. Employees are one of your most important assets; they can make or break your business. Your organizational skills for getting the product to market, managing other assets, and controlling cash flow will require constant attention.

In talking with hundreds of people interested in beginning their own businesses, I also discovered some common concerns. Perhaps you can identify with some of these.

What kind of business would I succeed at? There are three categories to consider: Manufacturing, retail, and service. Start with what you like and what you do best. Inventory your resources, both personal and financial, and identify your strengths and limitations. Think as a customer, and look for opportunities to apply your values and perspective.

Should I start from scratch or buy an existing business? Once again there are essentially three choices: Start from scratch, buy an existing business, or buy a franchise. The choice will be easier to make after you determine your goals, develop a plan, and inventory your resources.

Where can I get some money? This is probably the most common concern of the entrepreneur. It isn't as difficult as you might imagine—provided you have a clear goal and well-defined plans.

A major issue in the small-business community, whether buying, running, or selling a business is determining its "financial value." Market value may not be the same. The "market value" of any business is what buyers and sellers agree upon. The financial value is the ability of the business to generate future earnings. A business that is heavy in assets but light in earnings may have little financial value as a business but still have considerable market value. These concepts become important in either buying or selling a business.

Before investing your money in a business, it is wise to consider alternative opportunities. A properly-run business should net annual profits in excess of ten percent, after the owner has withdrawn wages. This compares favorably with other real estate or equity investments, but there is a risk element involved. Be aware of your tolerance for risk and take steps to ensure the safety of your principal.

Your own personal investment capital may not be sufficient to begin the business of your choice. If that is the case, then either reduce the scope of your choice or raise additional funds. Your choice may be too lofty at this point and should be redefined. When raising additional funds, always remember the difference between debt and equity. In exchanging outside money for a share of the ownership, you will have raised equity capital. By borrowing funds, you will have raised debt capital. The selection process should be weighed against the need of control in managing the business.

Having owned a business, you will realize that managing for success and profit may be totally different from what you had imagined. Devoting time to inventory and cash-management, dealing with personnel problems, keeping in touch with customer needs, marketing the merchandise or service, and staying competitive will test your imagination and management skills. You will receive immense satisfaction and personal growth from owning your own business. There is no better way to accumulate lasting wealth than in the execution of the "American Dream."

Finally, when you have attained your goals and are ready for another challenge, plan your exit as carefully as you planned your entrance into business. Selling your equity or liquidating the assets will be the final chapter of your successful career.